The Art of Scamming a Scammer

James Veitch

hachette
BOOKS

NEW YORK

Copyright © 2020 by James Veitch

Cover design by Nick Bilardello
Cover photograph © Matt Loxton

Cover copyright © 2020 by Hachette Book Group, Inc.

Hachette Book Group supports the right to free expression and the value of copyright. The purpose of copyright is to encourage writers and artists to produce the creative works that enrich our culture.

The scanning, uploading, and distribution of this book without permission is a theft of the author's intellectual property. If you would like permission to use material from the book (other than for review purposes), please contact permissions@hbgusa.com. Thank you for your support of the author's rights.

Hachette Books
Hachette Book Group
1290 Avenue of the Americas
New York, NY 10104
HachetteBooks.com
Twitter.com/HachetteBooks
Instagram.com/HachetteBooks

Originally published in 2015 by Quadrille Publishing in the UK.

First US Edition: June 2020

Published by Hachette Books, an imprint of Perseus Books, LLC, a subsidiary of Hachette Book Group, Inc. The Hachette Books name and logo is a trademark of the Hachette Book Group.

The Hachette Speakers Bureau provides a wide range of authors for speaking events. To find out more, go to www.hachettespeakersbureau.com or call (866) 376-6591.

The publisher is not responsible for websites (or their content) that are not owned by the publisher.

Picture credits:
Pages 19, 40, 56 inset, 57 inset, 58 inset, 60, 63, 66, 116, 126, 177 inset, 194 artwork by James Veitch; pages 54, 55, 56, 57, 58, 59, 119, 173 images emailed to James Veitch; page 118 © Steve McCabe; page 119 inset © David Turnley/Corbis

Library of Congress Control Number: 2020933661

ISBNs: 978-0-306-87459-8 (paper over board), 978-0-306-87458-1 (e-book)

Printed in the United States of America

LSC-C

10 9 8 7 6 5 4 3 2 1

Introduction

It was an email, received first thing in the morning from my friend Alex (unexpected trip, mugging), that sowed the seeds of what's become *Dot.Con*. It didn't take me long to realize it wasn't Alex (Western Union, alarm bells) and, I reasoned, this gave me the upper hand. I was sitting up in bed now, finger poised over *DELETE* on my iPhone when this question came quite unbidden: "What would happen if I replied?"

The marooned friend is one of the best known scams, principally because it's the one that dodges the spam filter most frequently. It comes from someone you know but, often, only tangentially. It's since become—hands down—one of my favorite scams. The scammer is pretending to be someone whom you know; they don't know how you know them, though, which means you can just make it up as you go along.

I pecked out a reply.

"What??????...Alex, but how on earth did this happen?"

And the game was afoot.

The correspondence lasted a day and forms the first section of this book. I had so much fun that it got me thinking: what would happen if I began replying to every scam email I received? And that's what I've been doing—for the past few years—on your behalf.

I've been inducted into the FBI, won the Peruvian lottery (twice), been buttered up by kings, princes and pirates. I have offshore accounts, consignments of gold and a serious girlfriend in Moscow.

Do try this at home; it's the only defense we have. But set up a pseudonymous email account and use that to reply. Initially, I was using my own account and, consequently, I think I was put on some sort of "list of suckers." I'd wake up to discover 400 new emails about penis enlargements, only one of which was a legitimate offer.

Don't get me wrong—I don't want to be mean to the scammers. There are lots of people online who do that. I'm content merely having fun inventing and I figure any time they're spending with me is time in which they're not scamming vulnerable adults out of their savings.

Incidentally, if you think you don't get spam, you do; you just have a very good spam filter. If you want to see what's been netted pre-inbox, open your spam folder—there be dragons...But also, I believe, opportunities. I think of the spam folder not as Pandora's box, but as a costume shop in which you can play and play at being whoever and whatever you wish. If only for a time. Last week, I was a bank robber, a pilot and the one-time confidant of a beautiful Arabian princess—and that was just Monday.

It's worth mentioning that for every one of the emails in the book, there were ten or twenty that didn't make the cut. Conversation would end abruptly when the scammer rumbled me as a time-waster, or an email would bounce, the scammer's email address having been confiscated and destroyed by their provider. More often than not, the scammer would refuse to go off-script, giving me just generic, pasted responses. But, on rare occasions, with enough coaxing...well, you'll see.

James Veitch

March 24, 2019
Manila, Philippines
(stranded following an unexpected trip)

The Poem

From: Alexandra K
To: James Veitch
Subject: Hi   Date: December 15 8:19 am

Hi, sorry to bother you but I made a trip early this week to London, UK and had my bag stolen with my passport and credit cards in it. The embassy is letting me fly without my passport, I just have to pay for a ticket and settle Hotel bills. I was thinking of asking you to lend me some funds. I need to be on the next available flight.

Alex

From: James Veitch
To: Alexandra K
Subject: Re: Hi   Date: December 15 9:56 am

What??????

From: Alexandra K
To: James Veitch
Subject: Re: Hi   Date: December 15 10:33 am

Thanks for your response i need $2000 to pay hotel bills and cover my expenses, let me know what you can come up with. I made inquires and was told western union would be the best option.

From: James Veitch
To: Alexandra K
Subject: Re: Hi   Date: December 15 3:54 pm

Alex,

But how on earth did this happen? I had no idea you were even in London? And two GRAND on hotel bills? How on earth did you manage that? You could have stayed at mine for free! I'm working on getting you the cash.

James

From: Alexandra K
To: James Veitch
Subject: Re: Hi   Date: December 15 3:59 pm

Thanks alot James i promise to pay back as soon as i get back. here are the details you will need in sending the funds via western union

Alexandra K,
Charing Cross Road,
London,
WC2H 0QU

From: James Veitch
To: Alexandra K
Subject: Re: Hi   Date: December 15 4:00 pm

To be honest, I'm a bit annoyed you've spent the past week in the lap of luxury and haven't contacted me at all. I thought we were close; what happened? Also, what's your room like? I'll talk to the bank tomorrow.

From: Alexandra K
To: James Veitch
Subject: Re: Hi   Date: December 15 4:05 pm

Dont be please you know my head was filled and i was a bit confused but now you promised to help my mind is at rest cant you be able to get the funds by today please i really need to get on the next avaiable flight let me know.

From: James Veitch
To: Alexandra K
Subject: Re: Hi   Date: December 15 4:08 pm

I know how you feel. If I'm paying the bill though do you think you could at least steal me some towels?

From: Alexandra K
To: James Veitch
Subject: Re: Hi   Date: December 15 4:48 pm

James try and get back to me with update let me know if you have sent the funds

From: James Veitch
To: Alexandra K
Subject: Re: Hi   Date: December 15 4:53 pm

Alex, before I do this, and I want to, but before I do this, just tell me one thing: how was I, as a lover? I've been wanting to know this for ages but haven't ever had the courage to ask.

From: Alexandra K

To: James Veitch

Subject: Re: Hi   Date: December 15 6:12 pm

James dont start am in a mess right now and my head aches please just get me out of this mess and we will discuss this when i get home okay,

Thanks and waiting to hear from you soon

From: James Veitch

To: Alexandra K

Subject: Re: Hi   Date: December 15 6:16 pm

If that's the way you're going to behave then maybe you can just dig yourself out of this mess. Remember Tuscany? Those huge waves? All I want to know is whether you still love me. Tell me you still love me?

From: Alexandra K

To: James Veitch

Subject: Re: Hi   Date: December 15 6:24 pm

Okay James i still remember the old times we spent together and i wish we could do it once more if we had the chance to okay i will never forget the good times we both spent together please just get me out of this mess

---

From: James Veitch

To: Alexandra K

Subject: Re: Hi   Date: December 15 6:31 pm

But do you love me???

From: Alexandra K

To: James Veitch

Subject: Re: Hi   Date: December 15 6:43 pm

yes i do love you James and i will meet you at the airport once
all this is clear okay so just get to a WU and wire the funds so
we can meet and spend time together all right. Keep me posted

Love you

From: James Veitch

To: Alexandra K

Subject: Re: Hi   Date: December 15 9:07 pm

Hi Alex,

Sorry, I've been busy all day today. I did manage to call my bank
to make sure I had enough money to cover the hotel bills. The
guy I spoke to said that Western Union isn't safe. Don't you think
it's better that we meet in person? On the way home I decided to
ask you to write me a poem. Nothing large; just a simple one, just
for me. Something about Tuscany. I remember writing you one all
those many years ago and you never replied to me. It would
mean a lot to me.

Yours, James

From: Alexandra K

To: James Veitch

Subject: Re: Hi   Date: December 15 9:09 pm

Western union is 100% safe okay all else you dont want to wire
the funds to me cause i made inquires and was told Western
union is the best way to receive funds fast and easier okay so if
are still willing to help me out of this just let know

From: James Veitch
To: Alexandra K

Subject: Re: Hi   Date: December 15 9:12 pm

And the poem?

From: Alexandra K
To: James Veitch

Subject: Re: Hi   Date: December 15 9:30 pm

I will write you the poem that is no problem but i need to get things straight first okay? wire the funds so i can get everything done and we can meet. do you still need the info's or you still have them

---

From: James Veitch
To: Alexandra K

Subject: Re: Hi   Date: December 15 10:31 pm

I'm not doing anything until I get a poem!

From: Alexandra K
To: James Veitch

Subject: Re: Hi   Date: December 15 10:58 pm

Fine i can see you are not helping matters thanks for your time

---

From: James Veitch
To: Alexandra K

Subject: Re: Hi   Date: December 15 11:06 pm

We'll always have Tuscany.

The Gold

To: James Veitch

Subject: (no subject)   Date: October 15 1:34 pm

Hello Mr. Veitch, How are you doing? Hope all is well with you.
I have an interesting business proposal I want to share with you.
I await your reply so that we can commence.

Regards, Solomon

From: James Veitch

To: Solomon Oddonkoh

Subject: Re: (no subject)   Date: October 15 7:54 pm

Solomon,

Your email intrigues me.

Go on. Go on.

Jim

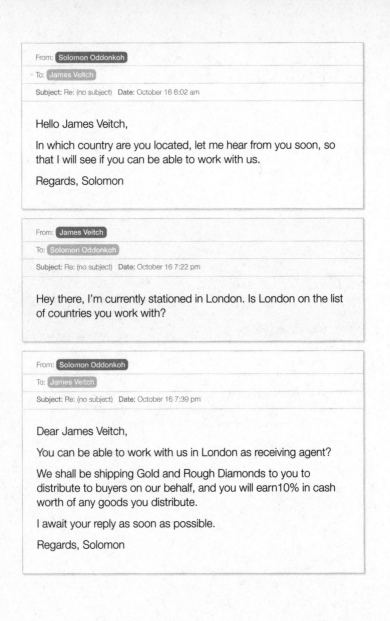

From: Solomon Oddonkoh
To: James Veitch
Subject: Re: (no subject)   Date: October 16 6:02 am

Hello James Veitch,

In which country are you located, let me hear from you soon, so that I will see if you can be able to work with us.

Regards, Solomon

From: James Veitch
To: Solomon Oddonkoh
Subject: Re: (no subject)   Date: October 16 7:22 pm

Hey there, I'm currently stationed in London. Is London on the list of countries you work with?

From: Solomon Oddonkoh
To: James Veitch
Subject: Re: (no subject)   Date: October 16 7:39 pm

Dear James Veitch,

You can be able to work with us in London as receiving agent?

We shall be shipping Gold and Rough Diamonds to you to distribute to buyers on our behalf, and you will earn10% in cash worth of any goods you distribute.

I await your reply as soon as possible.

Regards, Solomon

From: James Veitch
To: Solomon Oddonkoh
Subject: Re: (no subject)   Date: October 16 7:55 pm

Of course.

How much are they worth?

From: Solomon Oddonkoh
To: James Veitch
Subject: Re: (no subject)   Date: October 17 12:31 pm

We will start with smaller quantity of 25kgs of Gold as trial shipment.

The worth should be about $2.5million.

From: James Veitch
To: Solomon Oddonkoh
Subject: Re: (no subject)   Date: October 17 12:47 pm

Solomon, If we're going to do it. Let's go big. I can handle it.

How much gold and diamonds do you have?

From: Solomon Oddonkoh
To: James Veitch
Subject: Re: (no subject)   Date: October 17 1:12 pm

It is not matter of how much gold and diamonds that I have, what matters is your capability of handling.

We can start with 50kgs as trial shipment.

What do you do for a living?

50kg? You've got to be kidding me. There's no point doing this at all unless we're shipping at least a metric ton.

I'm a hedge fund executive bank manager so I know about these things. This isn't the first time I've shipped bullion my friend, no no.

Now. Where are you based? I don't know about you but I think, if we're going Royal Mail, it ought to be signed for—no?

It will not be easy to convince my company to do larger quantity shipment. We usually start with smaller quantity as trial shipment,

I am currently in Ghana. But we have mines all South America and Africa. Here is our www.katagoldd.web.com

---

Solomon, I'm completely with you on this one. We need to go into the meeting together and convince them that we need to ship three tons of gold.

I'm not talking about Spandau Ballet either.

Your website is down. Is that the right link?

I'm putting together a visual for you to take into the board meeting.

Hold tight.

From: James Veitch
To: Solomon Oddonkoh
Subject: Re: (no subject)   Date: October 17 4:58 pm

Solomon,

Attached to this email you'll find a helpful chart.

I had one of my assistants run the numbers and I've discovered an undeniable correlation between the amount of gold you and I have and our wealth.

For this reason, I think it's clear that we should be shipping as much gold as possible.

Let me know what your thinking is. See if you can get this by the board. Probably best you print out the attachment and take it in with you.

Images are powerful.

All best, James

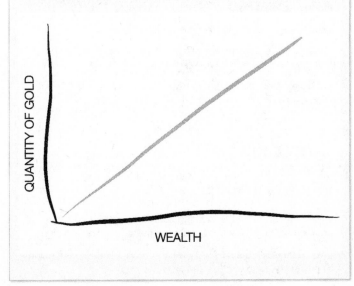

From: Solomon Oddonkoh
To: James Veitch
Subject: Re: (no subject) Date: October 17 5:16 pm

Okay Then you will have to call our marketing manager. And convince him about that.

From: James Veitch
To: Solomon Oddonkoh
Subject: Re: (no subject) Date: October 17 5:24 pm

No problem; I can call him in the morning. But I won't have the picture to show him. Could you be there so we can do a conference call? Sort of hit him with all the angles. You go in slow; I'll come in fast and heavy about the gold.

You're totally right about getting in touch with the manager of course. Here at the bank we, too, leave almost all major decisions to the marketing team.

How much room do you think the gold will take up?

There's not much room where I live. I can bin the microwave but that only frees up about two square feet.

Still trying to get on to your website; have you had your IT guys look at it?

From: Solomon Oddonkoh
To: James Veitch
Subject: Re: (no subject) Date: October 17 5:41 pm

If you can call him in the morning that will be great. I will get more details regarding the website from the manager in the morning.

I will be so much happy if the deal goes well, because I am going to get a very good commission as well.

From: James Veitch
To: Solomon Oddonkoh

Subject: Re: (no subject)   Date: October 17 6:10 pm

Superb. What's your cut if you don't mind my asking? Are you planning on spending it already? I want to get a new microwave. What's this guy's number?

James

From: Solomon Oddonkoh
To: James Veitch

Subject: Re: (no subject)   Date: October 17 6:23 pm

I will make $1000 commission per each kilo.
His phone numbers is +233-541370970. Name Wilson.

From: James Veitch
To: Solomon Oddonkoh

Subject: Re: (no subject)   Date: October 17 6:50 pm

Wow. See? We're both going to do all right out of this.

I'll call Wilson tomorrow morning.

What are you going to spend your cut on?

From: Solomon Oddonkoh
To: James Veitch

Subject: Re: (no subject)   Date: October 17 7:42 pm

On RealEstate, what about you?

From: James Veitch
To: Solomon Oddonkoh
Subject: Re: (no subject)   **Date:** October 17 7:57 pm

One word: hummus. It's going places.

I was in Sainsbury's the other day and there were about 30 different varieties.

Also, you can cut up carrots and dip them. Have you ever done that Solomon?

And peppers. The other day I got peppers of all different colors and cut them up and dipped them in hummus. Delicious. I've been eating a lot of cold food since the microwave packed in. Do you like microwaves? Will you have one in your new house?

From: Solomon Oddonkoh
To: James Veitch
Subject: Re: (no subject)   **Date:** October 17 9:59 pm

I have to go bed now. Till morrow. Have sweet dream.

From: James Veitch
To: Solomon Oddonkoh
Subject: Re: (no subject)   **Date:** October 17 10:02 pm

Bonsoir my golden nugget, bonsoir.

Subject: Re: (no subject) Date: October 18 12:11 pm

Solomon,

I had several meetings this morning and was unable to call the marketing manager.

Meanwhile, I'm concerned about security. The news tells us that the authorities are watching our every move. The other day I picked up my telephone and heard a *crackle* as I brought it to my ear. Then, as I was talking, there was a *popping* sound. Finally, when I put the receiver down, I heard a loud *snap*. The thought that someone could have been listening in put me right off my cereal.

Subject: Re: (no subject) Date: October 18 1:40 pm

All I need from you is to follow my instructions and I promise you we shall both smile at the end.

Subject: Security! Date: October 18 1:55 pm

Solomon,

Re. security: I think when we email each other, we should use some sort of code. Would that be all right? Say ok and I'll send you the code I've been working on.

James

To: James Veitch

Subject: Re: Security!   Date: October 18 3:43 pm

I agree totally that we should use a Code. Am sure from the coming week the Lawyer would have finished with the legal documents and we shall proceed with the claim process.

From: James Veitch

To: Solomon Oddonkoh

Subject: Re: Security!   Date: October 18 4:09 pm

Excellent. I spent all night coming up with this code; can we use it in all further communications please.

Bank: *Creme Egg*
Lawyer: *Gummy Bear*
Legal: *Fizzy Cola Bottle*
Claim: *Peanut M&Ms*
Documents: *Jelly Beans*
Western Union: *A Giant Gummy Lizard*

Please call me *KitKat* in all further correspondence.

The best thing to do is write the email and then go through it and replace all the terms with the ones I've provided. It would put my mind at rest and I think it would expedite the whole process. Looking forward to doing business with you!

KitKat

From: James Veitch

To: Solomon Oddonkoh

Subject: Re: Security!   Date: October 19 9:34 am

Solomon,

Is the deal still on?

KitKat

From: Solomon Oddonkoh
To: James Veitch
Subject: Re: Security!   Date: October 19 11:49 am

The Business is on and I am trying to raise the balance for the lawyer so that he can submit all the needed legal documents the bank for the claim process to start. Can you assist with some funds? Send to my name £1,500.00 via Western Union

---

From: James Veitch
To: Solomon Oddonkoh
Subject: Re: Security!   Date: October 19 1:13 pm

Solomon,

I certainly can. I can send funds tomorrow. But I'm very concerned about privacy. For instance in your email, "claim" should have been *Peanut M&Ms* and "documents" should have been *Jelly Beans*.

From: Solomon Oddonkoh
To: James Veitch
Subject: Re: Security!   Date: October 19 2:22 pm

The business is on. I am trying to raise the balance for the Gummy Bear so he can submit all the needed Fizzy Cola Bottle Jelly Beans to the Creme Egg for the Peanut M&Ms process to start. Can you assist with the funds? Send £1,500.00 via A Giant Gummy Lizard.

Solomon

From: James Veitch
To: Solomon Oddonkoh
Subject: Re: Security!   Date: October 19 2:25 pm

:)

The Snail Farm

Oramaeze Maxwell
@mormaeze

@veitchtweets I need an investor to invest 300000$ in farming that will yield profit of 6000000$ in eight months

09/29 01.04 pm

James Veitch
@veitchtweets

@moramaeze what sort of farming are we talking about? Will I need to milk a cow?

09/29 01.38 pm

Oramaeze Maxwell
@mormaeze

@veitchtweets no cow business but snail farm only

09/29 02.04 pm

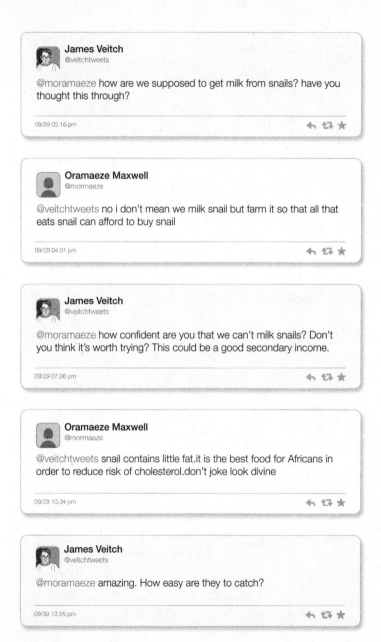

James Veitch
@veitchtweets

@moramaeze how are we supposed to get milk from snails? have you thought this through?

09/29 02.16 pm

Oramaeze Maxwell
@mormaeze

@veitchtweets no i don't mean we milk snail but farm it so that all that eats snail can afford to buy snail

09/29 04.01 pm

James Veitch
@veitchtweets

@moramaeze how confident are you that we can't milk snails? Don't you think it's worth trying? This could be a good secondary income.

09/29 07.06 pm

Oramaeze Maxwell
@mormaeze

@veitchtweets snail contains little fat.it is the best food for Africans in order to reduce risk of cholesterol.don't joke look divine

09/29 10.34 pm

James Veitch
@veitchtweets

@moramaeze amazing. How easy are they to catch?

09/30 12.56 pm

Oramaeze Maxwell
@mormaeze

@veitchtweets it is being hunt in the night because they move only in the night for food.

09/30 01.04 pm

James Veitch
@veitchtweets

@moramaeze gotcha. How fast do we have to be though? When I was younger I tried to catch a rabbit and it was very very hard.

09/30 01.07 pm

Oramaeze Maxwell
@mormaeze

@veitchtweets snail moves slowly

09/30 01.10 pm

James Veitch
@veitchtweets

@moramaeze how slowly?

09/30 01.13 pm

Oramaeze Maxwell
@mormaeze

@veitchtweets one of the most slow moving creature

09/30 01.32 pm

James Veitch
@veitchtweets

@moramaeze In principle, I'm in. How would you feel about coming in with me on a cheetah farm I'm planning?

10/03 05.58 pm

Oramaeze Maxwell
@mormaeze

@veitchtweets what next is to sign the contract legally and start construction of the farm.

10/03 07.16 pm

James Veitch
@veitchtweets

@moramaeze Question, how do we stop the snails escaping? could we organize some sort of ride around the farm or "park" for tourists?

10/03 07.32 pm

Oramaeze Maxwell
@mormaeze

@veitchtweets i have no fund for that.such farm better 4 western world

10/03 08.44 pm

James Veitch
@veitchtweets

@moramaeze not 100% sure Camden Council would grant planning permission for a snail farm. I had enough trouble getting resident's parking.

10/03 08.50 pm

James Veitch
@veitchtweets

@moramaeze Islington?

10/03 08.51 pm

Oramaeze Maxwell
@mormaeze

@veitchtweets snails will be controlled by a construction with wire gauge.hence no atom of risk involve.

10/03 11.17 pm

James Veitch
@veitchtweets

@moramaeze This wire gauge sounds perfect. Can we electrify it, too?

10/03 11.33 pm

Oramaeze Maxwell
@mormaeze

@veitchtweets no need

10/03 11.50 pm

James Veitch
@veitchtweets

@moramaeze Can we prevent a breakout though? What if something happens to the fences? What if the snails learn how to open doors?

10/04 07.41 am

Oramaeze Maxwell
@mormaeze

@veitchtweets security for all properties are my government first priority there is security provision in my proposal to you.no cause 4 fear

10/04 09.12 am

James Veitch
@veitchtweets

@moramaeze You say that but if we have a snail breakout it's not going to be as easy as when the Pirates of the Caribbean ride breaks down.

10/04 09.20 am

Oramaeze Maxwell
@mormaeze

@veitchtweets there is cause for alarm

10/04 01.18 pm

James Veitch
@veitchtweets

@moramaeze Exactly. We clocked the S African Snail going 32mm per hour.

10/04 01.44 pm

Oramaeze Maxwell
@mormaeze

@veitchtweets no escape

10/04 01.47 pm

James Veitch
@veitchtweets

@moramaeze What are we talking here? How many snails does £15 get me?

10/04 01.56 pm

Oramaeze Maxwell
@mormaeze

@veitchtweets i know the business very well as you know comedy very well

10/04 04.05 pm

James Veitch
@veitchtweets

@moramaeze If you know the snail racket half as well as I know callbacks, we'll be milking 'til kingdom come.

10/04 04.06 pm

Oramaeze Maxwell
@mormaeze

@veitchtweets the ball is in your court

10/04 04.07 pm

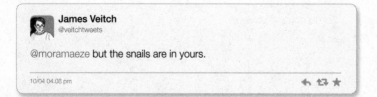

James Veitch
@veitchtweets

@moramaeze but the snails are in yours.

10/04 04.08 pm

The Blurb

From: Robert Fortnum

To: James Veitch

Subject: Need your help... Date: October 27 5:05 pm

Hello,

This message may be coming to you as a surprise but I need your help.Few days back my family and I made an unannounced vacation trip to Manila,Philippines. Everything was going fine until last night when we were mugged on our way back to the hotel. They Stole all our cash,credit cards and cellphone but thank God we still have our lives and passports safe.The hotel manager has been unhelpful to us for reasons i don't know.I'm writing you from a local library.

I've reported to the police and after writing down some statements that's the last i had from them.i contacted the consulate and all i keep hearing is they will get back to me. Our return flight leaves soon... I need you to help me out with a fast loan to settle our bills here so we can get back home i'll refund the money as soon as we get back.

Thanks, ROBERT

To: Robert Fortnum

Subject: Re: Need your help... Date: October 27 9:32 pm

Robert,

This is NO TIME to visit the library. Who's this hotel manager and why is he being so unhelpful?

Of course I'll loan you the money. What do you need? Shall I contact the consulate on your behalf?

How's Daphne?

James

From: Robert Fortnum

To: James Veitch

Subject: Re: Need your help... Date: October 28 10:12 am

Daphne's fine.

We are having such a frustrating ordeal here. I have nothing left on me except my passport which i could use as verification purpose at the Western Union outlet.

I'd really appreciate if you can loan me the cash. All i need now is $2,500 USD but will appreciate whatsoever you can afford to wired right now. You can send it via Western Union money transfer. I can receive the cash within minutes after it's sent using my International passport as identification.

Here is the information you need:

Name—ROBERT FORTNUM
Location: 54B Hilton Road, Makati City, Manila, Philippines
amount: $2500

Email me the transaction confirmation number as soon as it's sent. I promise to refund as soon as I arrive home.

From: James Veitch
To: Robert Fortnum
Subject: Re: Need your help... Date: October 28 2:30 pm

Of course Rob; you know I'd do anything for you and Daphne and the twins.

Let me check and see whether there's one of those Western Union thingies close by.

How soon do you need it?

James

From: Robert Fortnum
To: James Veitch
Subject: Re: Need your help... Date: October 28 2:45 pm

Thanks for your helping hand, i need the money urgently because i will need sort my bills, you can have the money wired online Via westernunion.com.

Let me know how much they charge in sending fee's so I can add to reimbursement.

Thanks, ROBERT

From: James Veitch
To: Robert Fortnum
Subject: Re: Need your help... Date: October 28 3:15 pm

Ok, ok.

I'm trying to get the cash out today but it's a Sunday so it's tricky. Doing my best for you buddy.

You haven't even asked how my writing is going!

James

OH,sorry i almost forgot to ask you how is your writing? i got lot thinking right now, i want to have the money wired to me online via westernunion.com if you can't locate any local store or WU outlet near you because i think having it done online would be more easier and faster.

Await your responds.

Thanks so much for asking, Robert. Just knowing you're out there—albeit in Manila—means a lot to me.

Actually I just checked online and there is a WU in central London that is open 24 hours so if I can convince my bank to let me get that much cash out, I'll go there this afternoon.

But did you end up finishing my novel? Last time we spoke you'd read half but not finished it. What did you think?

Tell Daphne we say hi.

Ok cool. Thank you for the help and we talk more once i arrive home. Keep me posted with the transaction confirmation number.

From: James Veitch
To: Robert Fortnum
Subject: Re: Need your help... Date: October 28 4:00 pm

Of course. But what did you think of the first 12 chapters of my novel? You know how important your feedback is to me.

From: Robert Fortnum
To: James Veitch
Subject: Re: Need your help... Date: October 28 4:12 pm

Well i appreciate every bit of what i read.

But i must let you know that am not in the mood for this now because we are really having such a frustrating ordeal here so it's not making me think well at all,so until i get home.

Hope you understand.

From: James Veitch
To: Robert Fortnum
Subject: Re: Need your help... Date: October 28 4:15 pm

Look Robbie, you're asking me for $2.5k but you can't even tell me what you thought of my novel? Take a moment, breathe a little and tell me your considered opinion.

I'm beginning to think you just don't care at all.

Yes i know it's been ages since we have a proper chat and i don't want you to think i don't care about your novel or maybe am feeling unconcerned about your novel but it's just we are a very bad and frustrating trip.

Just to let you to know that i really appreciate every bit of the wordings written on the novel. But the least i could say about the novel is that it's very passionate and sensitive.

Robster!

Thank you so much. I called my bank and they're making a one-time exception and allowing me to withdraw £2000. I need to tie up some business here and I may use your quotation for the back of the book; would that be all right?

One final question. How did you feel about the way it started? What did you think of the main character? And what was your favorite bit?

Please just tell me this and I'll go make the payment straight away.

Yours, James

From: **Robert Fortnum**

To: **James Veitch**

Subject: Re: Need your help... Date: October 28 4:47 pm

OMG What a million questions!!!

It's lovely and make's more meaning to someone life and i really love the way it started and what i think about the main character,lovely **Passionate and Sensitive,**

My favorite bit is just knowing that the novel has a lot and add alot to someone's life.

Please let me know what going on.

From: **James Veitch**

To: **Robert Fortnum**

Subject: Mock-up Date: October 28 5:54 pm

So sorry about all the questions. It means such a lot to me. I love that you described it that way.

I've attached a mock-up of the book that my publisher just sent me; I hope you don't mind but we used your quotation. What do you think? :) :)

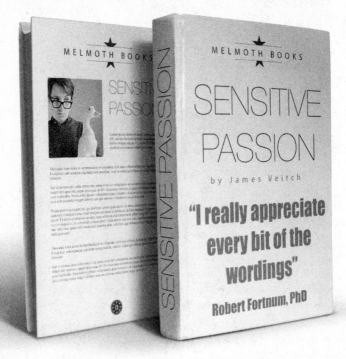

Wow this look good.

I will like you to go get the money sent now so i don't get frustrated.

From: James Veitch
To: Robert Fortnum
Subject: Re: Mock-up   Date: October 28 6:09 pm

I know, right?

Could you give me one more quotation for the back cover though, as my publisher is going nuts trying to get it out.

Just 30 words about the main plot twist and the bit with the robots and the milkmaid.

I just need to get this email sent off to her with the final changes and then I'll go to the WU to send your cash.

Cheers, James

P.S. Excited!!

From: Robert Fortnum
To: James Veitch
Subject: Re: Mock-up   Date: October 28 6:12 pm

Tired of your cunning.

OMG What a million questions!!! why you asking me this as at moment ?? Is this just because i asked you of help.. why have you decided to treat me like this, i want you to know that we're meant to help each other. I knew this is unusual but are the only person i could reach at this point and i'm doing everything i can so we can work our way out of here peacefully.

My flight leaves in hours from now and I really need your help to sort out the hotel bills. Kindly let me know if you're willing to help us out of this mess ok.

Of COURSE I am. But you've got to see it from my point of view; I haven't spoken to you in years, you email me out of the blue and ask for money. I've spent all day trying to get this money out of the bank (they even tried to tell me it was some sort of "scam") and now you tell me not only have you read my book but you LOVED it and you're willing to write me a blurb for the back cover.

Now my publisher is going nuts trying to get this 30 words and I'm just asking you for 30 words about the plot twist and the robots and the milkmaid before I head out the door. I swear I will get you this money within the hour. Just write me the blurb so I can shut my publisher up. You're the most respected Doctor of Philosophy in the country and I need your help, too.

Please, just gimme 30 words on *Sensitive Passion* and I'll send you the money.

OMG!!! why are you being so paranoid about this situation. I would never ask you to wire money to my name if i wasn't myself.

I never expected you could doubt me after explaining the horrible experience i went through,am seriously freaked out at the moment and need urgent help to get back home on time.

I'll be hanging on here to read from you soon.

OMG!! I can imagine. This is just how the milkmaid feels when she meets the robots in chapter 3.

I literally have the cash with me in crisp £10 notes. I just need to get to that Western Union but my publisher AND agent are now asking me for this blurb. Can you send now and then I will order a taxi to take me to the WU?

This novel is anincredible novel. The main character the milkmade is passionate and lovely and sensitive and the plot twist with the robots is good too.

This novel adds to peoples lives anyone who reads the book will be surprised by the twist. I also loved the way it started

ROBERT

Rob, this is beautiful. My publisher will be over the moon. I'm going to send you the money just as soon as the first royalty check comes in.

In the meantime, hang out in the library. It's a good place to be.

Tell No One

From: Juan Carlos
To: James Veitch
Subject: ATTENTION! Date: May 21 3:42 am

Greetings? Firstly, i must apologies for barge into your mailbox.
i seek a decision maker to grab 50% of $128 million. Yours free
Have i got your attention?
My question to you is do you want to be a millionaire? all you need
do is assist me on what is Required you get $64 million dollars
Have i got your attention?
I require UN undertaking that you will not run of with the money.
Driven by greed. call it winnings or compensation is your choice.
Have i got your attention?

From: James Veitch
To: Juan Carlos
Subject: Re: ATTENTION! Date: May 22 8:05 am

Sorry, can you repeat that? I wasn't paying attention.

From: Juan Carlos
To: James Veitch
Subject: Re: ATTENTION! Date: May 22 8:12 am

???

From: James Veitch
To: Juan Carlos
Subject: Re: ATTENTION! **Date:** May 22 8:29 am

Ok, I reread it and yes, in principle, I'm in. Very excited. Who am I allowed to tell about this?

From: Juan Carlos
To: James Veitch
Subject: Re: ATTENTION! **Date:** May 22 8:35 am

This transaction is a deal which you do no allowed to tell anybody. However, provide your personal information

---

From: James Veitch
To: Juan Carlos
Subject: Re: ATTENTION! **Date:** May 22 9:01 am

Ok. I'll be sending you my information in the next email.

Am I ok to tell my mother? She would be very excited to know that I was in such a lucrative business deal.

From: Juan Carlos
To: James Veitch
Subject: Re: ATTENTION! **Date:** May 22 9:58 am

Hello Mr. Veitch.

Yes, you can proceed and discuss this transaction with your mom so that she can partner with you and receive this $64 million.

i will be waiting for your information for we to start the transaction.

Mr. Jaun Carlos

From: **James Veitch**

To: **Juan Carlos**

Subject: Re: ATTENTION!   Date: May 22 12:04 pm

Wonderful. I've told my mother and she's very, very excited. She's asked me whether she can tell my uncle John about it. Is that ok? He might be coming in with us on the deal. I think we'll need help anyway because I don't work Mondays for obvious reasons.

From: **Juan Carlos**

To: **James Veitch**

Subject: Re: ATTENTION!   Date: May 22 12:50 pm

If you want to work with me and receive this money. let me know so that i can tell you more detail and procedures by which you have to follow.You can tell your uncle but no more.

From: **James Veitch**

To: **Juan Carlos**

Subject: Small prob   Date: May 22 7:27 pm

So my Aunty Norma was in the room when I told Uncle John about the $128 million. I remembered what you said and I told her not to tell anyone but she must have forgotten because she told Patrick who texted Aunt Molly and Uncle Nigel who conference-called Sue and Uncle Mark, Uncle Paul and Cousin Siobhan. Siobhan told Alan and Alan told Hannah and Hannah blabbed to Dan. Jeremy and Lorna know, too; I think Paul's to blame. And now they all want in. About the only person who doesn't know is Jonathan and that's only because he's in a different time zone.

The only good news is that Grandma's been told at least three times but still has no idea what we're on about.

Anyway, sorry for the hassle. I hope this doesn't affect the deal.

From: Juan Carlos
To: James Veitch

Subject: Re: Small prob   Date: May 23 4:22 am

You are warned to disregard other contact or any communication you have with other people from now henceforth.

From: James Veitch
To: Juan Carlos

Subject: Jonathan   Date: May 23 11:14 am

Jonathan knows. I don't know how, but he knows.

Genuinely really sorry about this.

From: Juan Carlos
To: James Veitch

Subject: Re: Jonathan   Date: May 23 1:40 pm

I contacted you based on Trust and confidentiality that you will keep this transaction as top secret and private.

From: James Veitch
To: Juan Carlos

Subject: Re: Jonathan   Date: May 23 1:56 pm

I don't see what the problem is. Thus far the only people who know are Mark, Paul, Siobhan, Grandma (sometimes), Patrick, Molly, Nigel, John, Norma, Jonathan, Hannah, Daniel, Jeremy, Lorna, Paul, Ma, Alan and me.

If poss, I'd like to keep this on the DL, so please don't tell anyone.

The Honey Trap

From: Elena
To: James Veitch
Subject: How did I find you?   Date: February 14 8:35 am

Don't wait far too long
tell someone how much you love,
and how much you care.

From: James Veitch
To: Elena
Subject: Re: How did I find you?   Date: February 14 6:21 pm

HAIKU!!! Send more.

From: Elena
To: James Veitch
Subject: Re: How did I find you?   Date: February 15 2:44 pm

My name is Elena.

i am searching for an understanding person who see love as the
only way of trust and care.

i have something important to tell you

From: James Veitch
To: Elena
Subject: Re: How did I find you?   Date: February 16 11:54 am

Elena,

That's SO weird. I was searching for an understanding person who see love as the only way of trust and care right when you emailed. What's this important thing you have to tell me?

I hate it when people do that because you could have just used the space you used to say "I have something important to tell you" to say the important thing itself.

James Veitch

From: Elena
To: James Veitch
Subject: About me   Date: February 17 1:21 pm

Dear James,

I am 24 years old, 5.6ft tall, never married before.

i am a girl who loves to give people happiness always despite what the circumstance might look like. Most of my hobbies are, reading novels, jogging, listening to music, cooking, listen to music, tv and movies.

I like honest, real, sincere and trustworthy people. But i hate dishonest, cheaters, and irresponsible peoples.

I have a cat. His name is Homka.

Elena

Let me introduce myself, too. I am Mr. James Veitch (rhymes with "peach"), 5'10" tall. I, too, have never married though my mother keeps asking probing questions about whether I've "met someone."

It's really nice to make your acquaintance. I, too, love movies and hate dishonest people! It's exciting to meet someone who shares the same esoteric range of likes and dislikes as I do.

I can't help noticing that you listed listening to music twice in your hobbies. Was this an oversight or are you just very passionate about listening to music?

My hobbies are playing piano and guitar, pining for girls, worrying about climate change, pining for girls and the poetry of John Keats.

Dearest James

I wish to let you know that sincerely is the best way in life. though we might be thousands of miles away from each other but it does not matter,what really matters in life is love not distance or color. I want to love and be loved.

Elena

Subject: Re: My life   **Date:** February 18 2:41 pm

Elena,

That's actually fairly beautiful. I think I read Fiona Apple said something like this recently. I'll try and fish out the quotation for you. Do you like the Beatles?

P.S. That's all I've *ever* wanted: to love and be loved.

Subject: Feelings   **Date:** February 19 6:23 am

I believe you are good and nice man. You are very Attractive Man.

I am excited and my head is like any big station with a lot of voice!

Subject: Re: Feelings   **Date:** February 19 1:49 pm

How long have you been hearing voices?

P.S. "Love is love, and there will never be too much."

Fiona Apple, *Letter to a Fan*

To: James Veitch

Subject: Re: Feelings   Date: February 20 2:36 pm

I like blue and red colors? What colors do you like?

If you don't mind to meet me please tell me the name of your city and nearest international airport! I will book my flight from Moscow.

I think you are interested that I don't have a boyfriend, because all men here look on my visual aspect and I want somebody who will look inside me.

From: James Veitch

To: Elena

Subject: Re: Feelings   Date: February 20 3:31 pm

I'm so sorry you haven't found anyone to look inside you yet. Come to London—I'll sort you out with an Oyster card.

In answer to your question, the nearest international airport is Heathrow. There's Gatwick, too but, to be honest, it's a pain in the ass. Don't ever get me started on Stansted. I'm quite excited to see you. But so soon? Do you normally fly out to meet someone you've just met??

James (call me Jimbo, please)

From: Elena

To: James Veitch

Subject: Re: Feelings   Date: February 21 1:57 pm

My honey Jimbo!!!!!!

I am glad that we have got acquainted in this big world of Internet and we can communicate here easyly now.

You are very attractive man.

Thanks so much for calling me Jimbo. It really makes me feel like we're becoming intimate. Albeit over the internet.

I'm just here in London. I live in a huge house but have it all to myself*. I have no family and am genuinely concerned about what will happen to all of my property when I shuffle off this mortal coil.

You'll have to be careful with me because I'm very forgetful and a bit eccentric. In essence, I've made a lot of money but have no one to spend it on. It just sits in a Swiss account earning interest. How boring! Don't go thinking I'm some sort of business mogul. I'm not; I've just made a few shrewd investments along the way (I bought hummus back in '93 when everyone was like "what's hummus?") and, as I say, I've had no one to share my wealth with.

So there; you've heard the good things about me. Here are some embarrassing things! I'm quite naïve and tremendously gullible. Really! My trusting nature has landed me in a pickle or two, I can tell you! I'm whimsical and spontaneous. I make rash decisions and I don't think about the consequences until afterward.

I hope none of this puts you off :(Tell me more about you. Who is your favorite Beatle? Mine's John. I am a very attractive man.

Hello my honey Jimbo! I already started my trip to you!

I still cannot believe I've done it!!!!!!!!!!!!!! Every my cell shouts about how it wants to see you. I do not want even to breath without you! I need you as an air.

I think that when a man and woman take the bath together it is very romantic. Would you like to take bath with me?

*Elena is dangling in front of me everything she thinks I want. Which makes me wonder whether I can return the favor. Who does Elena want? What's her ideal *mark*?

So glad to see your sweet name in my inbox once again. Every my cell shouts too! I wish you were here. I wish I had someone to share my life and wealth with; something to keep me from those bi-weekly money bonfires I have for tax purposes. I feel so alive!

But, Elena, the two-person bath isn't what they promise it's going to be. The only reason Julia Roberts and the guy could do it is because they were in a jacuzzi. Right from the start, they're a pain to coordinate and, once you're in, there's no space, hardly any water and your bum makes un-sexy squeaking noises as it rubs on the acrylic. And then you lie there waiting for one of you to admit that it isn't fun until the water gets cold. That said, if you want to have a bath with me, who am I to argue.

Your Jimbo, X

I am attaching a picture of me:

From: James Veitch
To: Elena
Subject: Re: Picture   **Date:** February 23 7:44 pm

Amazing! Which one are you?

From: Elena
To: James Veitch
Subject: Tickets   **Date:** February 24 12:15 am

I didn't guess that tickets costs so much. May be you could borrow some money?! You may send it by Western Union. It is pretty easy to use.

Here is a picture with your email address to show that I am real.

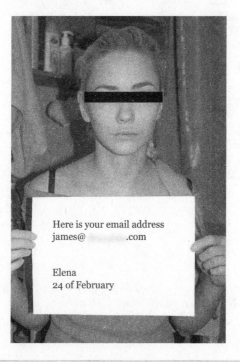

From: James Veitch
To: Elena
Subject: Re: Tickets   Date: February 24 12:23 pm

Love the picture. See attached! Will you bring Homka with you?

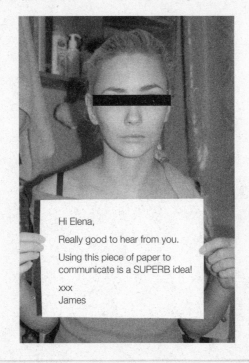

Hi Elena,

Really good to hear from you.

Using this piece of paper to communicate is a SUPERB idea!

xxx
James

From: Elena
To: James Veitch
Subject: So sorry   Date: February 24 8:38 pm

Without your help I will not be able to fly to you. But I do not want to be lonely again. I want you to warm your hands up in the back pockets of my jeans. I want you to love me.

I do no know homka. Who is homka?

Homka is your cat and, frankly, if you can forget about Homka so easily, what's to stop you forgetting about me?

But I want to see you, too. Not only do I want to warm my hands in the back pocket of your jeans but I get the distinct impression you would like to dip your hands into my back pocket, too.

Much love, James

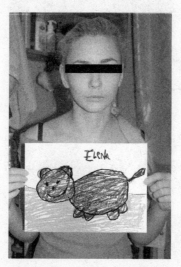

P.S. I improved your photo for you. See attached.
P.P.S. Somewhere, in Moscow, there is a hungry cat.

I do not wish to give you a words of good bye! If you cannot lend me money then I can not pay for a ticket. My last hope is you and only your kind and understanding heart.

Thoughts?

My Love! I have not understood your last letter! All my dreams is broken now. If i will not have money I should go home. I am crying everyday. I am ready to do everything to come to you and to see you. Please respond to my massage.

I loved your massage. But could we make a date further down the line? Perhaps September might suit? It all feels so rushed.

This is me and my passport.

From: James Veitch
To: Elena
Subject: Back at ya!   Date: February 26 11:59 am

This is really fun. Send me something else too! xxx

Mary Gary
Gary Mary

From: Mary Gary

To: James Veitch

Subject: Secret   Date: December 27 9:45 am

I am contacting you based on Trust and confidentiality that you will keep this as top secret.

From: James Veitch

To: Mary Gary

Subject: Re: Secret   Date: December 27 12:02 pm

I didn't read further than "trust" and "confidentiality."

I'm in.

From: Mary Gary
To: James Veitch
Subject: My story **Date:** December 27 1:20 pm

During a routine patrol by my unit sometime ago, I discovered a safe buried in a destroyed building. I inspect the safe and found it contained the sum of $15,000,000

But can I trust you? You take 40 percent and keep my 50 percent and donate 10 percent to charity organizations so that our good Lord will assist and bless us in future. I believe this is fair enough.

Your role is to find a safe place where it can be sent to. Can you handle these? We need to build trust. Do not let me down.

Mary Gary

From: James Veitch
To: Mary Gary
Subject: Re: My story **Date:** December 27 1:50 pm

Dear Gary,

I shan't let you down!

From: Mary Gary
To: James Veitch
Subject: Re: My story **Date:** December 28 8:29 am

My name is Mary Gary, feel free to call me Mary.

You must provide the following information: complete Names, Delivery Address, Occupation, Country.

I shall await your response. I am sending my Identification to you

M. Gary

From: James Veitch
To: Mary Gary

Subject: Re: My story   Date: December 28 4:00 pm

Gary, please find the info you need below.

Name: James Veitch
Address: Acacia Road W1 42S
Occupation: Fruit Consultant
Country: United Kingdom

From: Mary Gary
To: James Veitch

Subject: Re: My story   Date: December 29 3:07 am

It is Mary. my name is Mary Gary. There is no Gary unless it is my second name.

From: James Veitch
To: Mary Gary

Subject: Re: My story   Date: December 29 8:29 am

Ok. But if you're Mary, then who's this Gary? Are you sure we should involve a third person in this? Seems risky to me.

From: Mary Gary
To: James Veitch
Subject: Re: My story **Date:** December 29 9:51 am

It is only Mary. No Gary.

From: James Veitch
To: Mary Gary
Subject: Re: My story **Date:** December 29 1:34 pm

Ahhhhhhhhhhhhh. Gotcha.

From: Mary Gary
To: James Veitch
Subject: Re: My story **Date:** December 29 1:46 pm

Good.

From: James Veitch
To: Mary Gary
Subject: Re: My story **Date:** December 29 2:47 pm

Dear Mary and Gary,

Can you 100% confirm that this is real? I'm worried about scams.
All that Mary/Gary stuff got me a bit worried.

From: Mary Gary
To: James Veitch

Subject: Re: My story Date: December 30 11:44 am

This project is real, this transaction is no joke and such opportunity comes once in a life time. As stated in my last email to you, my name is Mary and Gary is my second name. Please remember.

Once again thank you and God bless America

From: James Veitch
To: Mary Gary

Subject: Re: My story Date: December 30 11:47 am

What's next?

From: Mary Gary
To: James Veitch

Subject: Re: My story Date: December 31 6:50 am

I must tell you about me. I love my husband and kids with great passion, but I lost them at the 9/11 bomb blast. I have given you my military id and like to see a picture of you too if you don't mind.

From: James Veitch
To: Mary Gary

Subject: Re: My story Date: December 31 6:55 am

I'm so sad to hear you lost your family during the 9/11 bomb blast. I lost many of my relatives during the bombing of the Titanic.

I don't have any photographs of me to hand but I'm attaching a portrait of me standing in front of my house.

Do not be alarmed; this is not to scale:

I must confess that I really appreciate your kind of person. I'll do all my possible best to make sure everything go smooth out here

The shipment will be tagged Ancient Graphic Art Materials and will be in Trunk Boxes. With this, it will not be checked at any port of entry by country customs or airport securities. So, it will be just you and me that is aware of its original content.

I trust in you, so please do not fail me or steal the money when it gets to you.

Ok. How much are these Ancient Graphic Art Materials worth?

From: Mary Gary

To: James Veitch

Subject: Re: Shipment Date: January 1 8:54 am

Please try to understand my previous message. The trunk boxes contains the sum of $15,000,000

From: James Veitch

To: Mary Gary

Subject: Re: Shipment Date: January 1 2:46 pm

But you just said they would contain Ancient Graphic Art.

From: Mary Gary

To: James Veitch

Subject: Re: Shipment Date: January 2 5:20 pm

The shipping company was told the trunk contains ancient graphic art, the company does not know the real content of the consignment, only you and i know that the trunk contains cash.

From: James Veitch

To: Mary Gary

Subject: Re: Shipment Date: January 3 5:45 pm

Gary, I just don't understand how ancient graphic art can be worth 15 million dollars. What am I meant to do with it?

From: **Mary Gary**

To: **James Veitch**

Subject: Re: Shipment Date: January 4 9:18 pm

Do you read my mails very well, if you do you would understand everything.

Listen my friend, the trunk boxes contains cash and not ancient graphic art okay.

From: **James Veitch**

To: **Mary Gary**

Subject: Re: Shipment Date: January 4 10:19 pm

Why didn't you say that before? This makes perfect sense now. I'm excited!

From: **Mary Gary**

To: **James Veitch**

Subject: Blessings Date: January 5 9:51 am

May the almighty God continue to guide and protect us in all our doings, I demand that, truth, honesty, sincererity and confidentiality should be our CODE WORD in this transaction.

From: **James Veitch**

To: **Mary Gary**

Subject: Re: Blessings Date: January 5 10:53 am

That's four code words. Which are we using?

May God Almighty help manifest a speedy transaction.

From: Mary Gary
To: James Veitch
Subject: Shipment dispatched   Date: January 5 9:11 pm

This is to inform you that the trunk boxes were dispatched some hours ago.

The shipping company charged $10,350 for diplomatic shipment. I had to remove the sum of $10,350 to complete payment for the charges. The total amount available in the trunk boxes after this deduction is now $14,989,650

The shipping company will contact you with the details

M. Gary

From: James Veitch
To: Mary Gary
Subject: Honesty   Date: January 5 10:42 pm

Sorry to be a dummy but I went for a cup of tea and when I got back to the computer I had forgotten what was in the trunk. Are you sending me a mix of money and graphic art or is the graphic art actually money or ancient money?

From: Mary Gary
To: James Veitch
Subject: Re: Honesty   Date: January 6 3:45 am

The consignment contains money and not ancient graphic art.

I had to lie to the shipping company so that they would believe the consignment contains ancient graphic art

This is to inform you that we have received a shipment of two trunk boxes and presently waiting for onward shipment to you.

Thanks Gaz.

I was really worried about the ancient graphic art. I've got a small apartment and nowhere really to display it. Unless I got rid of the toaster. But, it matters not because I've received an email from Airra Shipping.

Question. Do we need to give Mary a cut of the money too?

If at any time you are asked, just tell the shipping company the trunk boxes is full of ancient graphic art materials as indicated on the air way bill.

Please don't open the trunk boxes. There's no reason to. The trunk boxes is full of ancient graphic art materials as indicated on the air way bill.

From: AIRRA SHIPPING
To: James Veitch
Subject: Re: SHIPMENT RECEIVED **Date:** January 6 5:23 pm

We have received approval for your Non-Inspection Certificate at a cost of: $1085

From: James Veitch
To: AIRRA SHIPPING
Subject: Re: SHIPMENT RECEIVED **Date:** January 6 5:26 pm

No, there is nothing of interest for you inside the trunk boxes.

Being a dealer in Ancient Art and whatnot, I am accustomed to large shipments of this nature. There's nothing suspicious about that.

Ancient Graphic Art. That's my racket. And don't let anyone tell you otherwise.

From: AIRRA SHIPPING
To: James Veitch
Subject: Re: SHIPMENT RECEIVED **Date:** January 6 6:01 pm

You are required to immediately send the balance payment of $1085 for the The Non Inspection Certificate Fee This will enable the subsequent delivery of your trunk boxes to you.

From: James Veitch
To: AIRRA SHIPPING
Subject: Re: SHIPMENT RECEIVED **Date:** January 6 9:12 pm

These aren't the trunk boxes you're looking for.

You won't find anything anyway—apart from Ancient Art that's Graphic in nature.

From: AIRRA SHIPPING
To: James Veitch
Subject: Re: SHIPMENT RECEIVED   Date: January 7 12:59 pm

If you cannot meet up with the payment today, then the shipment
will have to be delayed.

From: James Veitch
To: AIRRA SHIPPING
Subject: Re: SHIPMENT RECEIVED   Date: January 7 3:06 pm

DO NOT UNDER ANY CIRCUMSTANCES LOOK INSIDE THE
TRUNK BOXES. I FORBID IT.

From: James Veitch
To: Mary Gary
Subject: Panic   Date: January 7 3:06 pm

Mary, how long do I need to keep up this ruse? I'm acting super
natural but I think they know something's up.

From: Mary Gary
To: James Veitch
Subject: Re: Panic   Date: January 7 3:36 pm

You should pay the fee they are asking for.

From: James Veitch
To: Mary Gary

Subject: Sincerity   Date: January 7 8:51 pm

I've been thinking about the percentages a lot. Could we do 40% for me, 50% for you, but also give 20% to charity? I don't feel like we're giving them enough in the current split.

From: Mary Gary
To: James Veitch

Subject: Re: Sincerity   Date: January 8 3:22 pm

i do not mind increasing the percentage to see the success of this,

---

From: James Veitch
To: Mary Gary

Subject: Confidentiality   Date: January 8 4:20 pm

This is fantastic. And I was also thinking that we should increase mine a bit too. Can we agree 40% for you, 65% for me and 20% to charity. Would that be ok?

From: Mary Gary
To: James Veitch

Subject: Re: Confidentiality   Date: January 8 5:15 pm

There is no problem my dear, am really worried about the consignment because of the much delay.

From: James Veitch
To: Mary Gary
Subject: Charley   Date: January 8 5:48 pm

If poss, I'd like to give my friend Charley one-fifth; he did Ancient
Greek at uni. Might come in handy with translating the Graphic Art.

From: Mary Gary
To: James Veitch
Subject: Re: Charley   Date: January 9 12:38 pm

Who is your friend you talk about and do you trust him?

From: James Veitch
To: Mary Gary
Subject: Final breakdown   Date: January 9 7:36 pm

FINAL BREAKDOWN
MARY: 40%
JAMES: 70%
CHARITY: 20%
CHARLEY: 1/5th
JAMES: 20%
and a further 35% for Gary?

From: Mary Gary
To: James Veitch
Subject: Re: Final breakdown   Date: January 9 8:03 pm

You have put your compensation two times.

From: James Veitch
To: Mary Gary

Subject: Re: Final breakdown   Date: January 9 9:34 pm

Damn, you're good.

From: Mary Gary
To: James Veitch

Subject: Re: Final breakdown   Date: January 10 8:13 pm

THe trunks are waiting for your payment. Do not delay.

From: James Veitch
To: Mary Gary

Subject: Question   Date: January 11 4:19 pm

Do we know what's in them yet?

From: Mary Gary
To: James Veitch

Subject: Re: Question   Date: January 12 2:59 pm

Do you think am kidding

From: James Veitch
To: Mary Gary

Subject: Re: Question   Date: January 12 3:00 pm

Do not think you're kidding.

Unless you are. Are you kidding?

Safety First

Sorry for any inconveniences, but I'm in a terrible situation. I came down here to Manila,Philippines. Last night I was robbed at gunpoint, my wallet and other valuables were stolen off me, leaving only my passport and life safe. My luggage is still in custody of the hotel management pending when I make payment on outstanding bills.

I need you to help me with a loan I will reimburse you soon as I get back Home.

All hopes on you.

Tom Beedham

Again??!! Noooo problem, Tom. What do you need this time?

From: Tom Beedham
To: James Veitch
Subject: Re: Reply ASAP...............Tom Beedham   Date: November 14 6:53 pm

Glad you replied. As soon as i get back home tomorrow i will definitely refund the money. All i need is £2,150 sent through western union to my information below.

Receivers Name: Tom Beedham
Location: Vicente Cruz Street 908, Espana, Near 7-Eleven
Manila City, 1000, Metro Manila

As soon as it is done, kindly get back to me with the western union confirmation number

---

From: James Veitch
To: Tom Beedham
Subject: Re: Reply ASAP...............Tom Beedham   Date: November 14 6:56 pm

Wow. That is a lot of money. Let me see what I can pull together. We may have to unplug Granny but I reckon it's doable :)

From: Tom Beedham
To: James Veitch
Subject: Re: Reply ASAP...............Tom Beedham   Date: November 14 7:27 pm

OK, Kindly go to the nearest Western Union Shop as soon as it is open tomorrow.

Keep me posted.

From: James Veitch
To: Tom Beedham
Subject: Re: Reply ASAP...............Tom Beedham   Date: November 15 9:25 am

Hey Buddy,

Just woke up. Had an awful nightmare about your gun mugging.
I'm a bit nervous about sending this much money abroad. Can I
just send it straight to your hotel?

From: Tom Beedham
To: James Veitch
Subject: Re: Reply ASAP...............Tom Beedham   Date: November 15 9:43 am

Hi,

The Hotel Management does not allow payment online only cash
in person.Kindly send via western union to my name and send me
the Money Transfer Control Number from western union(MTCN)#

Kindly do this and email me the transfer code ASAP.

From: James Veitch
To: Tom Beedham
Subject: Re: Reply ASAP...............Tom Beedham   Date: November 15 10:30 am

Boom! I sent the money and they gave me that confirmation
MTCN number you were on about.

From: Tom Beedham
To: James Veitch
Subject: Re: Reply ASAP...............Tom Beedham   Date: November 15 10:32 am

Send me the number please so I can pick up the money.

From: James Veitch

To: Tom Beedham

Subject: Re: Reply ASAP.................Tom Beedham   **Date:** November 15 10:40 am

Is it ok if I send the number to you in bits? It's a lot of money and I heard from a friend that emails can sometimes get hacked! Though, to be frank, that sounds far-fetched.

From: Tom Beedham

To: James Veitch

Subject: Re: Reply ASAP.................Tom Beedham   **Date:** November 15 10:40 am

Yes. Send in bits. Please quick.

From: James Veitch

To: Tom Beedham

Subject: Re: Reply ASAP.................Tom Beedham   **Date:** November 15 10:43 am

Ok, I'm really glad you agree about that. Incidentally, Lucy has had a baby. Can you believe it?! When did you guys break up again? Anyway, don't worry about that now. The first digit of the MTCN number to collect your cash is "1."

Reply back for the next bit. The baby has curly hair. Just like you.

From: Tom Beedham

To: James Veitch

Subject: Re: Reply ASAP.................Tom Beedham   **Date:** November 15 10:43 am

Send the number as whole number. This takes too long .

From: James Veitch
To: Tom Beedham
Subject: Re: Reply ASAP.............Tom Beedham **Date:** November 15 10:46 am

No, no no, we can't have this money going astray. Better safe than sorry. To be honest, that's a good rule of thumb generally. Re: Lucy, let me know if you need me to do a cheek swab.

Are you ready for the second number?

From: Tom Beedham
To: James Veitch
Subject: Re: Reply ASAP.............Tom Beedham **Date:** November 15 10:49 am

Yes please send more numbers though

From: James Veitch
To: Tom Beedham
Subject: Re: Reply ASAP.............Tom Beedham **Date:** November 15 11:05 am

Ok, I'll send two numbers this time to speed things up.

The next part is "23."

From: Tom Beedham
To: James Veitch
Subject: Re: Reply ASAP.............Tom Beedham **Date:** November 15 11:08 am

How many numbers altogether?

From: James Veitch
To: Tom Beedham
Subject: Re: Reply ASAP.................Tom Beedham Date: November 15 11:09 am

32

From: James Veitch
To: Tom Beedham
Subject: Re: Reply ASAP.................Tom Beedham Date: November 15 11:14 am

Tom?

From: Tom Beedham
To: James Veitch
Subject: Re: Reply ASAP.................Tom Beedham Date: November 15 11:16 am

Please give more numbers.

From: James Veitch
To: Tom Beedham
Subject: Re: Reply ASAP.................Tom Beedham Date: November 15 11:35 am

No can do. Security, Tom.

Are you ready for the fourth digit in the sequence?

From: Tom Beedham
To: James Veitch
Subject: Re: Reply ASAP.................Tom Beedham Date: November 15 11:40 am

Yes. I am ready.

From: **James Veitch**

To: **Tom Beedham**

Subject: Re: Reply ASAP............Tom Beedham   Date: November 15 12:03 pm

Ok, but just so I know it's still you, can you repeat back to me the numbers I've given you so far.

From: **Tom Beedham**

To: **James Veitch**

Subject: Re: Reply ASAP............Tom Beedham   Date: November 15 12:12 pm

You have given me 123

From: **James Veitch**

To: **Tom Beedham**

Subject: Re: Reply ASAP............Tom Beedham   Date: November 15 12:13 pm

CORRECT!

Ok. The next number is "4."

From: **Tom Beedham**

To: **James Veitch**

Subject: Re: Reply ASAP............Tom Beedham   Date: November 15 12:13 pm

Goodbye

From: **James Veitch**

To: **Tom Beedham**

Subject: Re: Reply ASAP............Tom Beedham   Date: November 15 12:15 pm

Ok. Let me know when you're ready for the other 28.

Devil Wife

From: John Kelly
To: James Veitch
Subject: John Kelly   Date: July 4 12:15 pm

I need your help.

From: James Veitch
To: John Kelly
Subject: Re: John Kelly   Date: July 4 8:24 pm

John! Why? Who are you?

Dear friend,

My name is John Kelly. I am 59 years old man.

I am in a hospital in Dubai. Recently, my Doctor told me that I would not last for the next six months due to my cancer problem (cancer of the lever)

I am giving my money away because of my health condition and the fact that my second wife is a terrifying woman to deal with, marrying her was the only mistake I made in my life.

She's currently managing my company here, but, I know what she's capable of, she has sold her soul to the devil and I do not want her to come near my money.

Regards, John Kelly

John,

I'm so sorry to hear of this. Cancer of the lever can be deadly.

Your second wife sounds awful. How did she sell her soul to the devil?

Are you sure it's your lever and not your second wife poisoning you? Make sure you check your food before you eat it.

James

From: **John Kelly**

To: **James Veitch**

Subject: Re: Dear friend   Date: July 5 7:04 am

Dear. James Veitch,

I am delighted to read your email. I must trust in you base on the information from you. My wife is a very wicked woman who want me death so that she can inherit my wealth.I am praying to God to extend my life.

John Kelly

From: **James Veitch**

To: **John Kelly**

Subject: Idea!   Date: July 5 1:55 pm

John,

I had an idea while I was in the bath this morning. When you sit down to dinner, say "look over there" or something and when she's looking the other direction, switch plates with her. That way if she's poisoned your food, she'll be eating it.

James Veitch

From: **John Kelly**

To: **James Veitch**

Subject: Re: Idea!   Date: July 5 4:25 pm

I feel sad when ever I talk about her. I need you sincere assistant to help me to move and invest the sum of nine million dollars.

Our business discussion must remain strictly confidential and my wife can never know about it.

From: James Veitch

To: John Kelly

Subject: Update Date: July 6 11:51 am

John,

Forget what I said before. Don't do the plate switcheroo. She's crafty. She might have anticipated the plate switching and already switched them. So don't switch the plates.

James Veitch

From: John Kelly

To: James Veitch

Subject: Re: Update Date: July 6 1:09 pm

Dear James Veitch,

Thank you for your kind advice. But I will also wish to remind you that I can only allow for 10 minutes by the doctor to check my email.

The funds are currently deposited with a private security company, your duty is to contact the company as my representative, arrange with them and finalize the funds into your account.

John Kelly

From: James Veitch

To: John Kelly

Subject: Ignore last email Date: July 7 11:25 am

I've had another bath and I think you should switch the plates. Hear me out: I think that she will have anticipated our anticipation and will give you the poison. Of course, it's quite possible that she might anticipate this though. Basically, I'm confused.

From: John Kelly
To: James Veitch
Subject: Re: Ignore last email   Date: July 7 12:19 pm

James Veitch you must inform me your readiness to allow me introduce you officially to the company as my financial investment representative

I wait for your approval

From: James Veitch
To: John Kelly
Subject: Re: Ignore last email   Date: July 7 11:24 pm

Of course, happy to help. Let me know the deets.

Meanwhile, my wife has been acting very strangely the last few months. I'm concerned she might be wanting me death too. It could be she's annoyed at the number of baths I've been taking. What are your top ten signs that your wife has become evil and wants your wealth?

From: John Kelly
To: James Veitch
Subject: Surgery   Date: July 8 10:38 am

James Veitch, I am going on a cancer surgery operation today.

Contact my lawyer with libbertylawfirm@hotmail.co.uk Tell him that I have willed 9.2M to you for the good work of the God, There might be a small processing fee

Dear Libberty Law,

John's having the op' today. Just in case things go pear-shaped, he's willed 9.2M to me to spend "as frivolously as possible."

Can you get in touch and let me know how I can best receive the money? I've run up a sizable water bill that I need to pay off asap.

All best, James

LibbertyLaw Chambers,
Sr. Corporate Legal Services
Malvern Terrace
London, UK

LibbertyLaw
Chambers

RE: BENEFICIARY FOR MR. JOHN KELLY ESTATE

Our client Mr.John Kelly has asked that we provide legal services on your behalf as his beneficiary in respect of funds ($9.2 Million)

We will require your personal information to prepare the required documents

Please send to this office the following details:

FULL NAMES, CONTACT ADDRESS, OCCUPATION, MONTHLY SALARY/INCOME, MARITAL STATUS, TEL/FAX NO, MOBILE PHONE NO.

I await your reply.

Regards, Barr.Libberty Moore
For: Libberty Chambers & Co

Dear Libberty Law,

YES. I am to be the beneficiary for John's estate.
Here are the details you asked for:

FULL NAMES: Alastair James Veitch
OCCUPATION: Hedge Fund Manager
MONTHLY SALARY/INCOME: ~ £40K
MOBILE PHONE NO: I don't trust the damn things.

How can I get this money? I'm so anxious to get a hold of it
I might just do something rash.

James

RE: BENEFICIARY FOR MR. JOHN KELLY ESTATE

Dear James Veitch,

We could not respond to your email yesterday because of the
news of John Kelly's death that reached us yesterday from Dubai
Mortality and Death Records Agency.

John Kelly passed out in the early hours of yesterday and his
remains have been deposited in a mortuary and will be burried on
the Monday next week in Dubai.

Get back to me so that I can instruct you on how you can send
the 900 USD to the court, for them to issue you the above
required documents for submission to the ING Bank for the
release of the funds to you. The bible made us to understand that
blessed is the hand that gives.

Barr.Libberty Moore

Dear Libberty Moore,

I am so sorry to hear that John Kelly has passed out. Do you mind my asking whether it was peaceful? It seems like I was talking to him only yesterday.

It's a shocking and entirely unexpected development. Begin with the wife. If you ask me there's something not quite right about her.

Meanwhile, I'm ready to receive the $9.2 million. I am so happy to do this. I am reminded of Psalms 13: 3–4 where the Lord says: "bring unto me the nine point two million in non sequential bills."

Please begin the transfer as soon as possible as I'm a bit impecunious just this minute.

James

RE: BENEFICIARY FOR MR. JOHN KELLY ESTATE

Dear James Veitch,

He died of complications resulting from the operation. May his gentle soul rest in peace.

You can send the payment for them to release of the funds to you.

From: **James Veitch**

To: **Libberty Law**

Subject: Re: Our Ref: L1311C/07   **Date:** July 11 6:21 pm

This must be hitting you hard then. How are you holding up?

I've been thinking it over and I couldn't, in all honesty, accept this money without knowing a bit more about John Kelly. Where is his funeral going to take place? I'm thinking of going.

J

From: **Libberty Law**

To: **James Veitch**

Subject: Re: Our Ref: L1311C/07   **Date:** July 12 2:17 pm

RE: BENEFICIARY FOR MR. JOHN KELLY ESTATE

We categorically stated that his remains would be buried on Monday in Dubai, which is today.

Thank you very much for your concern about my personal well being and how are you and your family doing? I hope great? May John Kelly's gentle soul rest in peace.

Yes, of a truth, his death is hitting me hard, and I am being able to hold up because of the actualization of his dreams that is near completion due to your kindness to assist him.

From: **James Veitch**

To: **Libberty Law**

Subject: Re: Our Ref: L1311C/07   **Date:** July 12 11:45 pm

Thank you and I'm sorry for missing that. I think I was in a state of shock when I read the email. Can you tell me a bit more about Dr. John Kelly—his life, his loves? Where were you when you found out about his passing out?

Subject: Re: Our Ref: L1311C/07   Date: July 13 9:19 pm

RE: BENEFICIARY FOR MR. JOHN KELLY ESTATE

I knew him very well as I was his company's lawyer here in the UK
when he was operating a super-market and a juice firm before he
sold them out and migrated to Dubai and ever since then, I have
been his personal lawyer.

Sequel to your second question, I have contacted the court and
I was told that the payment of 900 USD can only be effected via
the following stipulated and approved mode: *International Money
Transfer Agency*

Once this has been paid the $9.2 million will be released to you.

I await your reply.

Regards, Barr.Libberty Moore

Subject: Re: Our Ref: L1311C/07   Date: July 14 5:10 pm

Sorry I haven't gotten back to you; I've been in business meetings.
I wanted to tell you about a dream I had last night. You were in
it and John was in it, too. We were all there. You had 9.2 million
sheaves of corn that you were going to give me if only I gave you a
paltry 900 sheaves of corn. I handed you over my sheaves of corn
and, sipping his carton of supermarket orange juice, John smiled
at us in that sentimental, dewy-eyed way he always did. But when
I turned to look for you and your 9.2 million sheaves of corn, you
had vanished. I turned back to John but he merely shrugged his
shoulders and passed out again. Do you think it means anything?
Have you ever had dreams of this nature?

I'll go to Western Union in a few hours once I hear back from you.

Yours, James

RE: BENEFICIARY FOR MR. JOHN KELLY ESTATE

I wish to inform you that dreams often times are reflections of one's imaginations. Hence, I want to let you know that your dream is a mere reflection. Moreso, everything is in comformity with the laws and regulations of the judicial syetems here in the UK, so you do not have any cause to worry.

I await the payment immediately

Regards,
Barr.Libberty Moore

I hear what you're saying about dreams. You're so right. Anyway, as long as it's in conformity with the syetems then I'm on board.

One thing, though. I live in London you see, so I thought I'd just pop round and give you the $900 in person. Be good to meet up anyway and chew the fat. I stopped by your corporate offices in North London only I couldn't find an office there. Just a cul de sac. What's the deal?

All best, James

Sweet Rose

From: Godwin C
To: James Veitch

Subject: iPhone 4S 16GB Factory Unlocked   Date: April 4 11:41 pm

hello good day, how are you today? i saw the iPhone you put up for sale and i am interested in it, is it in good condition?

So tell me how much would it go for? You should come down a little bit on the prize,

I realy need this phone for my wife, and i can make payment as soon as possible.

From: James Veitch
To: Godwin C

Subject: Re: iPhone 4S 16GB Factory Unlocked   Date: April 5 9:23 am

The prize is £375.

From: Godwin C

To: James Veitch

Subject: Re: iPhone 4S 16GB Factory Unlocked   Date: April 5 2:10 pm

What matters now is that i told my wife and she like the phone

Ok, now i would like you to send it to my wife abroad she is a nurse and works with unicef, how is the cost of shipping?

God bless.

From: James Veitch

To: Godwin C

Subject: Re: iPhone 4S 16GB Factory Unlocked   Date: April 5 8:31 pm

That depends. What country would you like it shipped to?

From: Godwin C

To: James Veitch

Subject: Re: iPhone 4S 16GB Factory Unlocked   Date: April 6 6:56 am

Sorry for the delay i was at a meeting,, She is currently stationed in akure, ondo state, nigeria...How soon can you do that for me?

From: James Veitch

To: Godwin C

Subject: Re: iPhone 4S 16GB Factory Unlocked   Date: April 6 9:48 am

Immediately, my friend. Hope the meeting was ok.

From: **Godwin C**

To: James Veitch

Subject: Re: iPhone 4S 16GB Factory Unlocked   Date: April 6 11:55 am

Yes my friend the meeting was fine, thanks alot for asking, so i'll be expecting to hear from you soon, thank you...

From: **James Veitch**

To: Godwin C

Subject: Re: iPhone 4S 16GB Factory Unlocked   Date: April 6 3:56 pm

No problem. Just wing the PayPal over to this email and I'll send it out to your wife who is currently stationed in Nigeria.

Bless you.

From: **Godwin C**

To: James Veitch

Subject: Re: iPhone 4S 16GB Factory Unlocked   Date: April 6 8:13 pm

My friend i'm still with you ok, i am of to get your money ready ok,

From: **James Veitch**

To: Godwin C

Subject: Re: iPhone 4S 16GB Factory Unlocked   Date: April 6 9:19 pm

Good to know, Godwin. I'm still with you, too. Let's do lunch. We'll have shrimp.

From: Paypal

To: James Veitch

Subject: (no subject) Date: April 7 2:28 pm

---

service@intl.paypal.com <serviceonline@mail2online.com>
to me, bcc: me

PayPal

Dear Customer,
You have received an Instant Payment of £410. 00GBP from Mr Godwin C

Payment Details

Item Number	Item Title	Quantity	Price	Subtotal
Not Identify	Iphone 4	1	£375. 00	£375. 00

Note: Pls do ship today or tomorrow.		Shipping and handling	£15.00
I've sent payment for the phone...Thanks		Insurance	£0.00
		Total:	£410. 00GBP

From: Godwin C

To: James Veitch

Subject: Re: iPhone 4S 16GB Factory Unlocked Date: April 7 8:46 pm

My friend good evening, i have processed your paypal* so let me give you the actual address you will be sending it to. The manager of the hotel where my wife stays will receive it for her...

Name: Mr. Godfrey C
address: akarale road, akure, ondo state, nigeria

thank you and have a wonderful evening....

From: James Veitch

To: Godwin C

Subject: Re: iPhone 4S 16GB Factory Unlocked Date: April 7 9:20 pm

Godwin, 100% I'm with you on this one. I'm going to get this baby packaged up. Once I've done that, I'll ship it off to Nigeria.

What's your wife's name? How did you meet her?

---

*Godwin has sent me a phoney PayPal payment. The PayPal email looks legit until you look at the domain it's been sent from (top left)—@mail2online.com, which is definitely not PayPal.com. Godwin is betting on me not checking my PayPal account before I ship the phone. Which explains the urgency...

From: Godwin C
To: James Veitch

Subject: Re: iPhone 4S 16GB Factory Unlocked   Date: April 7 11:49 pm

My wife's name is Rose, but i fondly call her sweet rose because she is very pretty, i met her in 2008 when i went for my sister wedding ceremony in aberdeen.

From: James Veitch
To: Godwin C

Subject: Re: iPhone 4S 16GB Factory Unlocked   Date: April 8 12:30 pm

Aberdeen, Scotland? No WAY!

Godwin, lemme ask you a question. How do you show a girl you like her and are interested without scaring her away? What's your secret? I bet with Sweet Rose you behaved all nonchalant at first and that made her want you more. What's the secret, Godwin?

(iPhone is packaged.)

From: Godwin C
To: James Veitch

Subject: Re: iPhone 4S 16GB Factory Unlocked   Date: April 8 8:11 pm

James every lady likes a man that is bold, and goes directly for what he wants,

Do not worry so much over ladies. You will find a sweet rose of your own.

But you must scan and email me the shipping documents immediately.

From: James Veitch
To: Godwin C

Subject: Re: iPhone 4S 16GB Factory Unlocked   Date: April 9 9:02 am

Absolutely. I'm all over this, Godwin. You wouldn't believe how much I'm looking forward to sending my phone to you. I was thinking about what you said about girls and boldness all night. I think maybe the thing to do is to focus on other things and be independent; not *need* a lover. Then perhaps one will come along when I least expect it.

What's your favorite Beatles song and why?

From: Godwin C
To: James Veitch

Subject: Re: iPhone 4S 16GB Factory Unlocked   Date: April 9 11:42 am

Mr. James, realy i am not the type for music as it's not among my hobbies, i only come across the songs once in a while and i dont pay them attention...When do you intend to make the shipment?

From: James Veitch
To: Godwin C

Subject: Re: iPhone 4S 16GB Factory Unlocked   Date: April 9 11:59 am

Hey Godwin,

I packaged it all up yesterday, ready to go. You're not going to believe this but when I checked on it this morning, I discovered, to my dismay, that I didn't have an iPhone at all. What I actually had was just an old remote control for the television. God knows how I got it into my head that it was an iPhone 4. Does Sweet Rose need a remote control? If so, I can send it to you anyway.

James

The Sheriff and the Vacuum Cleaner*

From: Darrell K

To: James Veitch

Subject: 原來康康-這麼旺都是.半夜看A片   Date: April 2 2:30 pm

When you see vacuum cleaner around sheriff, it means that hand related to gets stinking drunk.

From: James Veitch

To: Darrell K

Subject: Re: 原來康康-這麼旺都是.半夜看A片   Date: April 2 2:31 pm

Darrell,

It's poetry, there's no doubt in my mind. But it needs formatting thus:

When you see vacuum cleaner around sheriff,
  it means
    that hand related to gets
stinking
drunk.

See? Far more accessible.

Send me some more of your stuff.

James.

---

*In 1996, someone wrote a tiny piece of software to generate (and then email) random, meaningless sentences. It's been running ever since.

Princess Mina

From: Princess Mina

To: James Veitch

Subject: how are you   Date: November 13 7:59 pm

hello how are you doing. I saw your email contact when i was searching for a friend in the internet.i will like to be your frined, I am in good health conditions and my body is healthy and no diseases in my body

my name is Princess Mina please i know you might not know me but i have a very important issue to discuss with you and i believe you can handle it

---

From: James Veitch

To: Princess Mina

Subject: Re: how are you   Date: January 9 7:37 pm

I'd love to be frineds with you. Where are you a Princess of?

You're right, I can handle it.

What is it though?

Subject: Re: how are you   Date: January 10 7:27 am

Hello James,

Thanks for responding to my message and how is weather over there in your country?

I am the only single daughter of my late Father who was Zimbabwe's main political power broker. My late father was imprisoned by Defense Minister Emmerson Mnangagwa, who is known as "the Crocodile." My late father is now dead.

Miss Princess Mina

From: James Veitch

To: Princess Mina

Subject: Re: how are you   Date: January 10 1:00 pm

Princess Mina,

I'm so sorry to hear about your late father but I'm sure your late father would be proud of you for raising the flag for your father who is late.

I have to tell you, I don't like the sound of this crocodile one bit. We must fight corruption wherever we find it! For example, I was at the optician's yesterday and the glasses weren't too pricey but then they tried to up-sell me on the thin lenses, reflective coating, Pentax anamorphic stuff. I know it's not quite the same, but I'm just trying to say that I get it, Princess Mina.

Question. Do you ever get tired of living in the palace? What's your day-to-day like? Do you have servants and a tiger?

Weather is fine.

James

From: **Princess Mina**

To: James Veitch

Subject: Re: how are you   Date: January 11 8:44 am

Oh James,

It is my pleasure to hear from you back! Life is hard for me here. My uncle was the one who have made every evil arrangement to kill my father. After my late father died, my uncle called a meeting on how to divert all my fathers investment. My uncle have asked my mother to hand him over all my late father's property document which include his industry called PAPER MILL INDUSTRY.

From: **James Veitch**

To: Princess Mina

Subject: Re: how are you   Date: January 11 10:33 am

Princess Mina,

This sounds awful. Oddly, I know a guy who was in a similar position and what he did was put a play on in front of his uncle. I know, I know—hear me out. You make the play about your uncle murdering your father. Your uncle will freak out when he sees it!

I'm sorry life is hard. What do you do to unwind? Do you have any pictures of you in royal attire?

P.S. One more thing: you might want to look into your mother's relationship with your uncle. No reason.

From: **Princess Mina**

To: James Veitch

Subject: Re: how are you   Date: January 13 1:06 pm

James, thank you for your words. The only thing i inherit from my father is the money. No one knows the existence of this deposit only the Reverend father and i will plead the man of God to release his personal phone number for me to pass it across to you...

From: James Veitch
To: Princess Mina

Subject: Re: how are you   Date: January 16 2:55 pm

You have God's personal phone number? Question. Is it 0870?
I don't care who he is; that's a very expensive call. Lots to chew
on here. What does PAPER MILL INDUSTRY produce?

From: Princess Mina
To: James Veitch

Subject: Re: how are you   Date: January 16 5:15 pm

hello dear, the PAPER MILL industry belongs to my late father they
produce stationary and toilet tissue papers but my wicked uncle
took over everything after master minding the death of my parents
and my brother. I know that he is behind all those calamities that
befall on my family.

From: James Veitch
To: Princess Mina

Subject: Re: how are you   Date: January 16 6:59 pm

Princess Mina, your story fills me with sadness. Have you tried
talking to your uncle? Sometimes that helps. Maybe if you told
him how upset you are that he masterminded the deaths of
your parents and brother it might clear the air. How is the loo roll
business going? Is he doing a good job of running that company?

From: Princess Mina
To: James Veitch

Subject: Re: how are you   Date: January 16 9:07 pm

my uncle is a very wicked and mean man, everybody fears him
whosoever that tries to stop him will pay with his or her life

From: James Veitch
To: Princess Mina
Subject: Re: how are you   **Date:** January 17 1:00 pm

Princess Mina, I would never betray you like your uncle has. But think about it from his perspective; he probably feels he has to live up to this image of him that you all have. He probably doesn't actually want to make people pay with their lives; he's just afraid of what would happen if, instead of executing them, he let them into his heart.

It's hard with family. I know this because I played Monopoly with mine at Christmas.

From: Princess Mina
To: James Veitch
Subject: Re: how are you   **Date:** January 17 3:02 pm

Before his death my father deposited a sum of 3.7 Million Dollars in leading bank in Europe with a strick instruction that the money will not be release unless;

1. I attain the age of 30 years or **2.** I am married to a man who is willing to love me **3.** I get a trusted partner or company. But right now i have not met any of these

---

From: James Veitch
To: Princess Mina
Subject: Re: how are you   **Date:** January 18 11:12 am

Have you thought about number 2? I could be willing to love you. I can't promise anything of course but you tick all the boxes. Together we can overthrow your tyrannical uncle and take over the family business. That is if he hasn't already flushed it down the toilet. Are you on Tinder?

From: Princess Mina

To: James Veitch

Subject: Re: how are you   Date: January 18 1:00 pm

I will accept that if you promise never to betray me. But first we must become business partners.

From: James Veitch

To: Princess Mina

Subject: Re: how are you   Date: January 18 1:46 pm

Wonderful news! I can't believe I'm getting married! Do you think we should invite your uncle to the wedding or is he persona non grata? Maybe we invite him to the dancing but tell him we're tight on numbers for the dinner and ceremony? That's a slap in the face.

From: Princess Mina

To: James Veitch

Subject: Re: how are you   Date: January 19 8:25 am

I am excited too my love.In this regard i will like you to contact the bank immediately and tell them that you are my foreign partner

---

From: James Veitch

To: Princess Mina

Subject: Some news   Date: March 3 3:42 pm

Oh Princess, there's no easy way to say this. I've met someone else. She's a bit all over the shop but falling, yes I am falling. Know that I'll always remember those first heady days when you were "in good health conditions and my body is healthy and no diseases in my body," and that rocky patch in January when we jilted your crazy uncle. James

The Toaster

From: Mrs. Debra Whitman

To: James Veitch

Subject: 45.3 million Pounds   Date: December 15 6:19 pm

Greetings to you in the Name of Our Lord and Savior Jesus Christ,

My late husband deposited the sum of £45.3 million Poundswith a Bank in India. I do not know when my time will be up, it might be shorter than the doctors said or more if God willing.

I saw your profile on Microsoft EMAIL owners list and picked youbecause i know in my heart you can be trusted. I am Mrs. Debra Whitman a 82 years old woman, married to a citizen who till his death was a reputable businessman in Isle of Man.

Isle of Man, is otherwise known simply as Mann, is a selfgoverning British Crown Dependency, located in the Irish Sea. The head of state is Queen Elizabeth II, who holds the title of Lord of Mann.

Best Regards, Debra Whitman

From: James Veitch
To: Mrs. Debra Whitman
Subject: Re: 45.3 million Pounds   Date: December 15 8:24 pm

Greetings to you too.

Honestly, being on that Microsoft EMAIL owners list has been such a blessing. I'm so glad I signed up for it.

Tell me more about this Isle of Man or "Mann," as you call it.

Of course I am happy to help. How can you get the money to me? It's a huge amount of money; I'm concerned about it going into my bank account.

James

From: Mrs. Debra Whitman
To: James Veitch
Subject: Re: 45.3 million Pounds   Date: December 15 9:11 pm

Hello James

The Isle of Man is more or less as England is in the UK, just that England is the Capital. There is Scotland and Ireland too.

I want you to use the fund to setup an orphanage with 70% of the total funds and the rest 30% keep that for yourself. My preliminary thoughts are to focus on children, the elderly and homelessness.

It was Google email owner list I got your email from actually.

Debra Whitman.

Subject: Re: 45.3 million Pounds   Date: December 16 8:17 am

Ah. I am on both lists, so that makes sense. Tell me more of the Isle of Man. Where does Guernsey fit in?

I'm with you 100% on this orphanage home. Where is it going to be and what shall we call it? I'm going to brainstorm this afternoon. You do it, too and let me know what you come up with.

You say that your preliminary thoughts are on the children, the elderly and homelessness. That's a fairly broad scope, Deb, and I really think we should focus on just one of those to start with. Otherwise we risk spreading ourselves too thin. Also, what if we take in a homeless child or a homeless old person or even an old, homeless child? Do they get triple the attention? We really need to think about these things.

Jim

From: Mrs. Debra Whitman

To: James Veitch

Subject: Re: 45.3 million Pounds   Date: December 16 11:45 am

Dear JAMES. The capital of Guernsey is Saint Peter Port, while the capital of Isle of Man is Douglas. Scotland capital is Edinburgh.

The location and name of the home is your responsibility. The bank will request Activation fee for new account. I will wait for you email.

Debra Whitman

From: James Veitch
To: Mrs. Debra Whitman
Subject: Re: 45.3 million Pounds **Date:** December 16 6:22 pm

Debbie, of course I can make contact with the bank today and set up a new account. There's an offer of a free toaster on at the moment and I've got my heart set on it.

Your geography is superb btw.

From: Mrs. Debra Whitman
To: James Veitch
Subject: Re: 45.3 million Pounds **Date:** December 17 10:24 am

Hi James, very good to know you can contact the bank immediately.

I do not understand what you meant by "There's an offer of a free toaster on at the moment and I've got my heart set on it" can you explain?

please get back, thanks, Debra.

From: James Veitch
To: Mrs. Debra Whitman
Subject: Re: 45.3 million Pounds **Date:** December 17 11:02 am

Defo. Basically the whole toaster thing works like this: the bank gives me a free toaster as a "thank you" for starting an account.

Would you want the toaster or could I keep it?

From: **Mrs. Debra Whitman**

To: **James Veitch**

Subject: Re: 45.3 million Pounds   Date: December 17 1:19 pm

Don't worry about getting a toaster.

Please contact info@royalbs.co.in don't delay. My health is not too good now. I don't have much days here on Earth.

From: **James Veitch**

To: **Mrs. Debra Whitman**

Subject: Re: 45.3 million Pounds   Date: December 17 1:59 pm

D, it's all very well for you to say "don't worry about getting a toaster," but how am I supposed to warm my bread?

So sorry to hear about your health. It sounds like you are not long for this mortal coil. On the plus side, though, you couldn't be handing over your £45.3 million to a more trustworthy individual. Sure, I have a penchant for fast cars and gold tiaras, but I'm also all about the little things—like the toaster.

When are you leaving Earth??

From: **Mrs. Debra Whitman**

To: **James Veitch**

Subject: Re: 45.3 million Pounds   Date: December 17 3:10 pm

dont let the time I'm leaving earth be of more concern to you,..

From: James Veitch
To: Mrs. Debra Whitman

Subject: Re: 45.3 million Pounds   Date: December 17 3:20 pm

Debra, I'm worried that we'll be in business together and then one day you'll just up and leave Earth without giving me any notice.

Is this not a valid concern?

From: Mrs. Debra Whitman
To: James Veitch

Subject: Re: 45.3 million Pounds   Date: December 17 5:05 pm

if you no longer read from me then it has happened.

From: James Veitch
To: Mrs. Debra Whitman

Subject: Re: 45.3 million Pounds   Date: December 18 11:40 am

Will you tell me before the countdown begins?

From: Mrs. Debra Whitman
To: James Veitch

Subject: Re: 45.3 million Pounds   Date: December 18 12:44 pm

I have not seen anybody that is more unserious as you are.

Even if I will die soon, do you have to mock me with it? just go ahead and get the funds to the bank

Debra.

From: James Veitch
To: Mrs. Debra Whitman
Subject: Re: 45.3 million Pounds **Date:** December 19 11:38 am

Debra, I had no idea we were talking about your death!

Meanwhile, have you given any thought to the name of the orphanage? I was thinking we could call it:

James and Deb's home for needy old homeless children

Or is that not catchy enough? What are your thoughts?

From: Mrs. Debra Whitman
To: James Veitch
Subject: Re: 45.3 million Pounds **Date:** December 19 11:40 am

What were you thinking I was talking about when I said I will be leaving this earth, am I going to Mass?

From: James Veitch
To: Mrs. Debra Whitman
Subject: Re: 45.3 million Pounds **Date:** December 19 11:41 am

Where's Mass? Is that where the toaster is?

From: Mrs. Debra Whitman
To: James Veitch
Subject: Re: 45.3 million Pounds **Date:** December 19 11:44 am

Sorry I mean Mars one of the planet of the Nine planets of the solar system.

From: **James Veitch**
To: **Mrs. Debra Whitman**

Subject: Re: 45.3 million Pounds   Date: December 19 11:48 am

Are we counting Pluto, then? If so, are you sitting down?
I have some news.

From: **James Veitch**
To: **info@royalbs.cn.in**

Subject: Hi   Date: December 20 10:55 am

Dear Royal Bank of Scotland*, I'm writing to you about some
money Debbie Whitman is leaving me. She mentioned something
about a free toaster. Can you confirm?

From: **© Royal Bank of Scotland ®**
To: **James Veitch**

Subject: Re: Hi   Date: December 20 12:40 pm

Please fill in the account opening form. There is no free toaster.

Raj.
Head of costumer care, Royal Bank of Scotland

From: **James Veitch**
To: **© Royal Bank of Scotland ®**

Subject: Re: Hi   Date: December 20 4:48 pm

Dear Costumer care, are you sure? I heard I was getting a free gift
for opening the account. Also, what sort of costumes do you do?
I've always wanted a proper Bananaman one.

---

*These guys are masquerading as the Royal Bank of Scotland. What I love is that their
email address is info@royalBS.

From:	© Royal Bank of Scotland ®
To:	James Veitch
Subject: Re: Hi	Date: December 21 11:14 am

No Sir, there is no bonanza going on.

From:	James Veitch
To:	© Royal Bank of Scotland ®
Subject: Re: Hi	Date: December 21 11:16 am

And there was I thinking you were having a bonanza over there.

Serious question. Have you ever had a bonanza at the bank or am I barking up the wrong tree?

From:	© Royal Bank of Scotland ®
To:	James Veitch
Subject: Re: Hi	Date: December 21 1:20 pm

No we had not, and even if we had there will be conditions applied.

James or whatever your name may be, stop playing with us This bank has every good reason to believe you are a scam, trying to lure Mrs. Debra Whitman into giving you her inheritance

From: James Veitch
To: © Royal Bank of Scotland ®

Subject: Re: Hi   Date: December 21 2:44 pm

"There is no free toaster."
Then how do you explain this??

From: © Royal Bank of Scotland ®
To: James Veitch

Subject: Re: Hi   Date: December 22 1:57 pm

that do not include Royal bank of Scotland Group Worldwide
I'm sorry you are disappointed not getting a free Toaster.

From: James Veitch
To: © Royal Bank of Scotland ®

Subject: Re: Hi   Date: December 22 2:20 pm

That's ok. I understand. What can you provide instead of a
toaster? I could do with a new kettle.

From: © Royal Bank of Scotland ®
To: James Veitch
Subject: Re: Hi Date: December 23 9:28 am

Sir, please be informed that there is no give away gift of any kind.
This bank have not done bonanza of any kind for a long time. We
will appreciate it if you do not bring up any issue regarding this gift
thing again because you won't get any.

From: James Veitch
To: © Royal Bank of Scotland ®
Subject: Re: Hi Date: December 23 12:07 pm

Ok. I shan't bring it up again. But just to be clear: are you saying
that if I bring it up again I won't get any and that if I don't bring it
up again I will? Or are you just saying that I won't get any at all?

From: © Royal Bank of Scotland ®
To: James Veitch
Subject: Re: Hi Date: December 23 3:19 pm

Please stop talking of a free toaster.

From: James Veitch
To: © Royal Bank of Scotland ®
Subject: Re: Hi Date: December 24 12:34 pm

I am so sorry about all this malarkey with the toaster. I shan't
mention the toaster again. You have my word.

What we want from you is to do the right things, and print out the form, fill it and sign and after filling send us a scanned copy of the form, and your ID.

I've done some research and I think the one we should go for is the DeLonghi 4-slicer in red.

Winnie

From: Winnie Mandela

To: James Veitch

Subject: (no subject) Date: March 1 9:31 pm

I AM WINNIE MANDELA. I AM THE SECOND WIFE OF NELSON MANDELA THE FORMER SOUTH AFRICAN PRESIDENT. HOW ARE YOU TODAY?

I AM IN POSSESSION OF US$45 MILLION DOLLARS. I NEED TO TRANSFER IT OUT OF THE COUNTRY BECAUSE OF MY HUSBAND MR. NELSON MANDELA'S HEALTH CONDITION.

IF ALSO HAVE A GOOD BUSINESS IDEAS ON ANY LUCRATIVE INVESTMENTS, I WILL MAKE YOU INVESTMENTS MANAGER.

ONE LOVE

YOURS TRUELY, MRS. WINNIE MADIKIZELA MANDELA

From: James Veitch
To: Winnie Mandela

Subject: Re: (no subject) **Date:** March 3 10:20 pm

So sorry to hear of this. Given that Nelson died three months ago I'd describe his health condition as fairly serious.

Nevertheless, I have some great ideas for investments :)

Tell me a story about Nelson? What did he like for breakfast?

James

From: Winnie Mandela
To: James Veitch

Subject: Re: (no subject) **Date:** March 3 10:38 pm

Nelson is now a history.

We will speak on investing my money afterward. Kindly comply with my banker for the transfer to be done smoothly.

From: James Veitch
To: Winnie Mandela

Subject: Re: (no subject) **Date:** March 3 10:40 pm

Not Cheerios then? Can you just tell me if it's Cheerios? I'd like to eat the same thing as him.

From: Winnie Mandela
To: James Veitch

Subject: Re: (no subject) **Date:** March 3 10:42 pm

The bank needs transfer fee of us$3800 dollars for the transfer to be made to your account.

To: Winnie Mandela

Subject: Re: (no subject) Date: March 3 10:43 pm

I'm going to assume it's Cheerios.

From: Winnie Mandela

To: James Veitch

Subject: Re: (no subject) Date: March 3 10:55 pm

dont ask me stupid questions.

if you are here for jokes stop further communicating with me here because i dont have time for this foolishness.

From: James Veitch

To: Winnie Mandela

Subject: Re: (no subject) Date: March 4 11:16 am

I don't like the way you're talking to me one bit. Is this how you used to talk to Nelson?

From: Winnie Mandela

To: James Veitch

Subject: Re: (no subject) Date: March 4 6:11 pm

Remember i will offer you 25% of the fund

ONE LOVE

From: James Veitch

To: Winnie Mandela

Subject: Re: (no subject)   Date: March 4 6:16 pm

Awesome.

NO WOMAN NO CRY

From: Winnie Mandela

To: James Veitch

Subject: Re: (no subject)   Date: March 4 6:18 pm

This is 11.3 Million Dollars

ONE LOVE

From: James Veitch

To: Winnie Mandela

Subject: Re: (no subject)   Date: March 4 6:19 pm

Amazing!

I SHOT THE SHERIFF
(But I did not shoot the deputy)

From: Winnie Mandela

To: James Veitch

Subject: Re: (no subject)   Date: March 4 6:20 pm

And I will make you my investment manager if you have a good idea for investments

I would LOVE to be your investments manager. I haven't done much of it before but I've got some rock-solid ideas I think you'd love to hear. Many of them involve the chickpea.

I am praying that the transaction will be smoothly accomplished. Please assure me you will not betray me in this transaction.

Winnie (may I call you that?), I agree. The transaction should be done smoothly. On that note, I've actually been making smoothies in the mornings—crushing up cashew nuts and almonds and adding oats and banana etc.—the sort of thing Nelson always liked for breakfast. They're so delicious and healthy. Essentially, what I'm saying, Winnie, is that you and I could do worse than to consider getting into the smoothie business.

We could call it *Winnie & James's Smoothies*.

Also, hummus; it's going places.

From: James Veitch
To: Winnie Mandela

Subject: Re: (no subject)   Date: March 4 8:10 pm

When do you want to meet? I can't do this weekend,
unfortunately. I'm seeing a show then going dancing. Unless
you wanted to come. What are your thoughts?

From: Winnie Mandela
To: James Veitch

Subject: Re: (no subject)   Date: March 4 8:35 pm

what do you mean by seeing a show then going dancing ?

From: James Veitch
To: Winnie Mandela

Subject: Re: (no subject)   Date: March 4 9:09 pm

Would you prefer something more low-key like roller-disco? I've
literally always wanted to do that.

From: Winnie Mandela
To: James Veitch

Subject: Re: (no subject)   Date: March 4 9:41 pm

EXPLAIN MORE BETTER TO ME ON WHAT YOU ACTUALLY
IMPLYING HERE: low-key like roller-disco?

From: James Veitch
To: Winnie Mandela
Subject: Re: (no subject)   Date: March 5 8:46 pm

I don't know, Winnie. I'm playing jazz! Also, marketing idea below. Thoughts? Just say what you think.

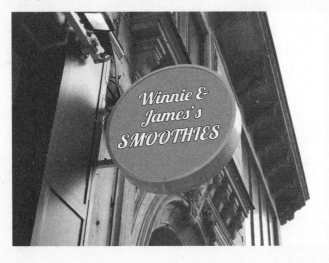

From: Winnie Mandela
To: James Veitch
Subject: Re: (no subject)   Date: March 5 9:48 pm

i can only visit you when the transfer is completed.

I'll make the transfer this evening on my way home. But Winnie, do you ever feel like we should do something more with our lives? Not just this ramshackleness and chasing girls.

In the middle of the night do you ever turn the pillow over, feel its coolness on your cheek and think, "it's the little things"?

i am the formal first lady to my late husband nelson Mandela. how could you be asking me such a foolish queries.

W, I don't think this is working out. I can't find any houses in our price range. London is so expensive. Moreover, I went to the bank to see about getting a mortgage and I had a number in my head and the mortgage guy had another number in his head and, as it turns out, those were different numbers. His was actually a minus number.

In these situations I often ask myself, "what would Nelson do?" and the answer is, almost always, move slightly further outside London for cheaper prices.

You knew him best. Would he consider Aylesbury?

Keith

From: Catherine H.

From: Catherine H.

To: James Veitch

Subject: (no subject)   Date: December 17 5:22 pm

Dear James.

I could not inform anyone about our trip, because it was impromptu. we had to be in Manila, Philippines for a program. Our journey has turned sour. we misplaced our wallet, passport and cell phone.

I will be indeed very grateful if i can get a loan of 1,800 Euro from you. I promise to refund it in full as soon as I return

Catherine

From: James Veitch

To: Catherine H.

Subject: Re: (no subject)   Date: December 17 6:12 pm

Catherine,

Of course I can help you out. What happened? Is everything ok? How's Keith doing?

From: Catherine H.

To: James Veitch

Subject: Re: (no subject)   **Date:** December 17 6:24 pm

James!

Am so glad you replied back..... Let me know if you are heading to the Western Union outlet now...

From: James Veitch

To: Catherine H.

Subject: Re: (no subject)   **Date:** December 17 6:34 pm

Of course. Don't worry. How's Keith though?

From: Catherine H.

To: James Veitch

Subject: Re: (no subject)   **Date:** December 17 6:49 pm

James, Keith is Fine please let me know. He's having a meeting with the british embassy now to get replacement passports. Please go to the western union. I owe you A lot...

Catherine

From: James Veitch

To: Catherine H.

Subject: Re: (no subject)   **Date:** December 17 7:01 pm

Cat, I'll pop along first thing tomorrow.

I must say though, Keith seems remarkably capable for a Yorkshire terrier. Last I remember he could roll over and woof for a treat; now you say he's taking meetings at the British embassy? What are you feeding him???

China Jewellery Corporation

From: China Jewellery Corporation

To: James Veitch

Subject: Your registration request received   Date: November 20 5:38 pm

Greetings Dear Candidate,

I found your CV in the Internet, and after reviewing it, we would like to offer you a Regional Manager position with our recently formed European department. There is no formal Interview process for this position and most of communication is done on-line.

Here is the position summary:

Position: *Regional Manager*
Base Remuneration: *2,950 EUR per month plus bonuses*
Available in: *UK, Portugal, Denmark*

This is a home-based position, which means that you will be working remotely, online. Let us know when you can start.

Sorry for using Gmail address for communication, the company e-mail address will be provided in further communications.

Sincerely, Dominic Farnham
HR department

Dominic,

Sorry it took so long to get back to you. For some bizarre reason, your legitimate job offer ended up in my spam folder!

Great news about my C.V. I'm really glad I slapped that bad boy on the internet. What sort of job is it? I'm quite handy with a spanner.

I must confess, I like the cut of China Jewellery Corporation's jib. Most other "companies" I've applied to make you jump through all sorts of hoops: references, interviews, applications etc. Most even demand you meet face to face. Ridiculous, right?

Anyway, full disclosure: Denmark is off the cards for me for obvious reasons.

The salary is quite sufficient but it would be churlish not to haggle. I'll take 2985 EUR per month and not a penny less. And I don't work Tuesdays for obvious reasons. Are we agreed?

Yours, James Veitch
Regional Manager CHINA JEWELLERY CORPORATION

James

We will be transferring money into your bank account. Your main job will be withdrawing the funds from your bank and transferring them using Western Union.

Best Regards, Dominic Farnham
HR Coordinator

From: James Veitch
To: China Jewellery Corporation

Subject: Your newest employee! Date: November 27 4:11 pm

Dominic,

This sounds like a great position!

I'm currently between jobs right now so I think I can make it work. One thing: I don't work Wednesdays for obvious reasons.

Best Regards, James Veitch
Regional Manager CHINA JEWELLERY CORPORATION

P.S. Does it matter that I have a criminal record?

From: China Jewellery Corporation
To: James Veitch

Subject: Re: Your newest employee! Date: November 27 4:12 pm

Your crime was what

From: James Veitch
To: China Jewellery Corporation

Subject: Re: Your newest employee! Date: November 27 4:12 pm

Embezzlement from a jewelry firm.

From: China Jewellery Corporation
To: James Veitch

Subject: Re: Your newest employee! Date: November 27 4:13 pm

Not matter

From: James Veitch
To: China Jewellery Corporation

Subject: Re: Your newest employee! Date: November 27 5:20 pm

Excellent! All in the past anyway*.

This sounds like the sort of gig I can really get my teeth into. On that note, question: do you provide any form of dental insurance?

Jim

*fairly recently

From: China Jewellery Corporation
To: James Veitch

Subject: Re: Your newest employee! Date: November 27 5:25 pm

No, unfortunately we don't provide dental insurance.

From: James Veitch
To: China Jewellery Corporation

Subject: Secretary Date: November 27 5:29 pm

Not a dealbreaker. I'll just have to brush more :)

I'll obviously need a secretary. Is it ok if we hire my sister, Louise? She's a hard worker.

From: China Jewellery Corporation
To: James Veitch

Subject: Re: Secretary Date: November 28 2:17 pm

You can hire any body you want to be your secretary at your own expense.

To: China Jewellery Corporation

Subject: Re: Secretary   Date: November 28 3:23 pm

Good to know, Dom. I've gone ahead and hired Louise. She wants to know whether there's a dental plan. I told her there wasn't one but can you please just reiterate to me that there is no dental plan?

Louise: "*I can't believe* there's no dental plan."

J

From: China Jewellery Corporation

To: James Veitch

Subject: Re: Secretary   Date: November 29 12:56 pm

THERE IS NO DENTAL

From: James Veitch

To: China Jewellery Corporation

Subject: Re: Secretary   Date: November 29 1:04 pm

Gotcha. Thing is, Dom, Louise is actually quite hard to work with. We may have made a mistake hiring her in the first place.

I'll keep you posted.

JV

To: James Veitch

Subject: Re: Secretary   Date: November 29 2:00 pm

You must send us your ID proving your identity, preferably a copy of valid Passport or DL. We require this for background check.

Sincerely, Dominic Farnham

From: James Veitch

To: China Jewellery Corporation

Subject: A few minor concerns   Date: November 30 3:16 pm

Domanac,

This whole Louise thing isn't working out. She takes a two-hour lunch break and, frankly, I can't stand staring at her crooked teeth all day.

If only we had supplied dental. Is it ok to give her the boot? I'm going to hire my friend Thelma instead. She has nicer teeth and is, on the whole, more reliable.

From: China Jewellery Corporation

To: James Veitch

Subject: Re: A few minor concerns   Date: November 30 3:20 pm

Mr. Veitch,

You can hire any one you want but you must send us your passport before we can pay your salary. Please be serious with us.

From: James Veitch
To: China Jewellery Corporation
Subject: Not good news   Date: December 1 11:40 am

Bad news, Domonoc. Louise has gone on strike over the lack of dental and Thema's useless.

I asked her to make a scan of my passport and send it to you a few days ago and I'm nearly 100% certain she didn't do it. I'm thinking of forgetting about this whole secretary business altogether.

From: China Jewellery Corporation
To: James Veitch
Subject: Re: Not good news   Date: December 1 11:45 am

We have not received passport. Please be serious with us. We have many other candidates for the position at CHINA JEWELLERY CORPORATION. You must do as we say.

From: James Veitch
To: China Jewellery Corporation
Subject: Resignation   Date: December 3 5:34 pm

We're in bad shape here, Dom.

We needed some fresh blood so I hired Nigel as the new secretary. But this really pissed off Thelma and Louise who began picketing the offices over the absence of dental insurance. Now they've gone off on some sort of crazy road trip.

I hereby tender my resignation. It's been a blast. Nigel's doing his best but he's only 12 years old so he finds it a bit overwhelming.

James Veitch
Former Regional Manager
CHINA JEWELLERY CORPORATION

Hong Kong

From: Cho Mak
From: Cho Mak

To: James Veitch

Subject: Mrs. Cho Mak   Date: January 5 12:04 pm

I am Mrs. Cho Mak, a staff of Dahsong Bank Hong Kong. I would like to intimate you with certain facts that I believe would be of interest to you.

From: James Veitch

To: Cho Mak

Subject: Re: Mrs. Cho Mak   Date: January 5 1:01 pm

Intimate away!

From: Cho Mak
To: James Veitch
Subject: Re: Mrs. Cho Mak   Date: January 6 6:04 am

Thank you for giving me your time, Let me start by introducing myself, I am Mrs. Cho Mak, a staff of Dahsong Bank Hong Kong.

A client deposited 13.9 million dollars in an account at the Dahsong bank. I was the officer assigned to his case; a few months later he was apparently dead and he listed no next of kin.

My proposal; I will nominate you as the next of kin and have them release the deposit to you. Upon receipt of the deposit, we share the proceeds 50/50.

Yours Sincerely, Mrs. Cho Mak.

From: James Veitch
To: Cho Mak
Subject: Re: Mrs. Cho Mak   Date: January 6 11:33 am

Intimate no more. I am your man.

But Cho (may I call you Cho?), how can I pass for your client? What's his name?

Question. Will I need to grow a mustache?

From: Cho Mak
To: James Veitch
Subject: Re: Mrs. Cho Mak   Date: January 7 7:12 am

Call me Cho. I am very glad to note that you are a noble, matured, and trustworthy person. I will do everything legally required to ensure that the project goes smoothly.

You do not need to grow a mustache.

Mrs. Cho Mak.

From: **James Veitch**

To: **Cho Mak**

Subject: Re: Mrs. Cho Mak Date: January 7 12:26 pm

I'm going to try and grow one anyway. One can never be too careful, Cho.

Meanwhile, do you think I should come to Hong Kong? How long does the transaction last? Will I have time to take in some of the sights? If so, what do you recommend? Bear in mind I get bored really easily.

From: **Cho Mak**

To: **James Veitch**

Subject: Re: Mrs. Cho Mak Date: January 8 5:10 am

Dear James Veitch,

Coming to hong kong is not the problem, but first this task must be completed before planing to come to hong kong, and when this task is completed i will be glad to welcome you to hong kong. Please do you know that this is a laudable transaction we are into,

---

From: **James Veitch**

To: **Cho Mak**

Subject: Re: Mrs. Cho Mak Date: January 8 7:20 pm

Cho, I've looked at tickets and they're pretty pricey. Cheeky question, but could I stay with you so I don't have to get a hotel? Happy with sofa.

From: **Cho Mak**

To: **James Veitch**

Subject: Re: Mrs. Cho Mak   Date: January 9 4:22 pm

There is no need to come to Hong Kong. i do not mean you should come and see me I was expecting to receive a scan copy of your identity

---

From: **James Veitch**

To: **Cho Mak**

Subject: Re: Mrs. Cho Mak   Date: January 9 4:38 pm

I'm not terribly good at computers, so I've been having some difficulty getting you a scanned copy of my ID. But I bought a laudable scanner on the internet and it should arrive soon.

The good news is that I'm pretty much packed. Can you confirm that they have KitKats over there? I'm partial to them and if they don't, I'm going to have to bring my own.

From: **Cho Mak**

To: **James Veitch**

Subject: Re: Mrs. Cho Mak   Date: January 10 7:24 am

Dear James Veitch,

Thank you for your prompt response, you are free to bring whatsoever you want to bring, there are kit kats,

Please can you send me all the information on your international passport or drivers license. You do not have to travel to anywhere for any reason. I shall await for your Update.

From: James Veitch
To: Cho Mak

Subject: Re: Mrs. Cho Mak   Date: January 10 9:40 am

Wonderful news about the KitKats. Here is my info as requested:

Name: Alastair James Bruce Veitch
Sex: Not for a while
Date of Birth: 01/04/1980
Nationality: British

From: Cho Mak
To: James Veitch

Subject: Re: Mrs. Cho Mak   Date: January 10 2:33 pm

Dear James Veitch,

I have got your information, and I will be sending them all to the lawyer. I will further update you later on the bank where you are to open a new bank account in your name

---

From: James Veitch
To: Cho Mak

Subject: Re: Mrs. Cho Mak   Date: January 10 4:19 pm

One can never have enough bank accounts—that's what I say.
I just wanted to check that it's still ok to stay at yours? Just FYI I'll be bringing three small dogs.

From: Cho Mak
To: James Veitch

Subject: Re: Mrs. Cho Mak   Date: January 10 4:20 pm

PLEASE DO NOT COME TO HONG KONG

From:	James Veitch
To:	Cho Mak

Subject: Big news!   Date: January 16 5:05 pm

I'm here! In Hong Kong! Arrived today and having the time of my life. Wow, it's big here! Where's the best place to meet?

Got to go; I thought this was an internet café but it's just someone's house.

Excited!

From:	James Veitch
To:	Cho Mak

Subject: Small problem   Date: January 17 9:31 am

Having some difficulty finding you. It transpires that Cho isn't as uncommon a name as I believed it to be. I'm going to pop into the Dahsong Bank HQ and see if they can page you.

Sayonara!!!!

From:	Cho Mak
To:	James Veitch

Subject: Re: Small problem   Date: January 17 11:42 am

I am not in HongKong. I have traveled for the western part of the world as part of my bank work I will not be there for two weeks. I told you not to come to Hong Kong. And you have not contacted the bank.. James Veitch why are you herre?

From: **James Veitch**
To: Cho Mak

Subject: Re: Small problem   Date: January 19 1:30 pm

Must have just missed you!

Should I wait? I've made a load of friends so I could probably hold out for a while until you're back from the western part of the world.

From: **Cho Mak**
To: ~~James Veitch~~

Subject: Re: Small problem   Date: January 20 12:15 pm

Do not wait for me. i have spent thousands of hong kong dollars on this transaction. Please try as much as you can to set up this account as soon as possible, so we could finalize this this week:

Mr. Charles Frankfort / csu@i-santander.co.uk
General Director of Operations, i-Santander Bank

From: **James Veitch**
To: Cho Mak   i-Santander Bank

Subject: Phew!   Date: January 22 11:38 am

Back now. Exhausted. But thanks for the info; so glad to be opening an account with good old *i-Santander*. I'll get in touch with them right now.

From: **James Veitch**
To: i-Santander Bank

Subject: Bank account   Date: January 25 11:40 am

Dear i-Santander,

I'd love to open an account, please. I'm going to be investing a considerable sum very soon.

Subject: Internal Office Memo   Date: January 26 6:37 am

WELCOME TO I-SANTANDER BANK 24/7 ONLINE SERVICE

Internal Office Memo

Dear Customer,
Sequel to your correspondence please endeavor to state
clearly the exact type of account you desire

1. Savings Plus Reserve Account:
*Account features; *Requires Account Opening/Setup Deposit of **650.00***
***Great British ponds** (GBP) *24/7 Online Banking Direct Access*
**Maximum transfer: 1,000,000.00 GBP monthly.*

2. Current Plus Reserve Account:
*Account features; *Requires Account Opening/Setup Deposit of **1,600.00***
***Great British ponds** (GBP) *24/7 Online Banking Direct Access*
**Maximum transfer: 2,000,000.00 GBP monthly.*

3. Advantage Gold Reserve Account:
*Account features; *Requires Account Opening/Setup Deposit of **3,800.00***
***Great British ponds** (GBP) *24/7 Online Banking Direct Access*
**Maximum transfer: 3,000,000.00 monthly.*

4. Diamond Reserve Account:
*Account features; *Requires Account Opening/Setup Deposit of **5,200.00***
***Great British ponds** (GBP) *24/7 Online Banking Direct Access *No maximum*
transfer limits. (This means you can Transfer Any Possible Amount at Once)

Subject: Re: Internal Office Memo   Date: January 29 11:43 am

Great to hear from you. I don't ask much in a bank, but I do
view the sharing of internal office memos with customers as an
absolute prerequisite.

Anyway, sequel to that, I'd like to go for the **Savings Plus
Reserve** Account. Pond for Pond, it seems like the best bang
for my buck.

From: i-Santander Bank

To: James Veitch

Subject: Internal Office Memo   Date: January 30 8:47 am

Internal Office Memo
Congratulations on choosing the *Savings Plus Reserve Account*!
Please make the payment of £650 required for the activation of
your *Savings Plus Reserve Account*

Mr. Charles Frankfort

From: James Veitch

To: i-Santander Bank

Subject: Re: Internal Office Memo   Date: February 2 1:48 pm

I've changed my mind. I'd like to go with the **Current Plus
Reserve Account**. The 1 million GBP limit of the **Savings Plus
Reserve Account** is a real bottleneck for me.

Can we commence this as soon as possible, please? I don't have
much days here on Earth.

From: i-Santander Bank

To: James Veitch

Subject: Internal Office Memo   Date: February 3 7:14 am

Internal Office Memo
Congratulations on choosing the *Current Plus Reserve Account*!
Please make the payment of £1600 required for the activation of
your *Current Plus Reserve Account*

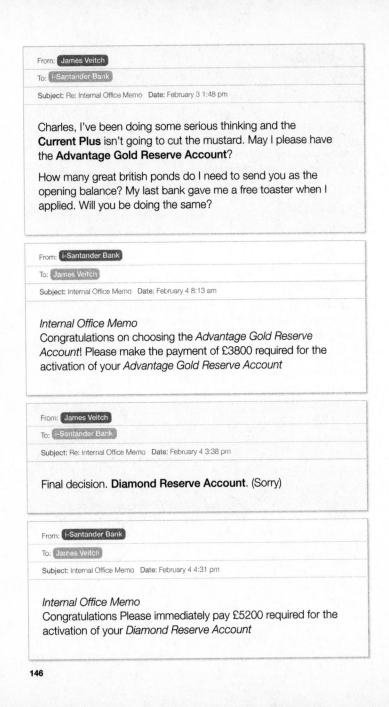

From: James Veitch
To: i-Santander Bank
Subject: Re: Internal Office Memo   Date: February 3 1:48 pm

Charles, I've been doing some serious thinking and the **Current Plus** isn't going to cut the mustard. May I please have the **Advantage Gold Reserve Account**?

How many great british ponds do I need to send you as the opening balance? My last bank gave me a free toaster when I applied. Will you be doing the same?

From: i-Santander Bank
To: James Veitch
Subject: Internal Office Memo   Date: February 4 8:13 am

Internal Office Memo
Congratulations on choosing the *Advantage Gold Reserve Account*! Please make the payment of £3800 required for the activation of your *Advantage Gold Reserve Account*

From: James Veitch
To: i-Santander Bank
Subject: Re: Internal Office Memo   Date: February 4 3:38 pm

Final decision. **Diamond Reserve Account**. (Sorry)

From: i-Santander Bank
To: James Veitch
Subject: Internal Office Memo   Date: February 4 4:31 pm

Internal Office Memo
Congratulations Please immediately pay £5200 required for the activation of your *Diamond Reserve Account*

From: James Veitch
To: i-Santander Bank

Subject: Re: Internal Office Memo   Date: February 4 10:22 pm

Chaz, you think I should have stuck with the **Current Plus Reserve Account**, don't you? Be honest. I think I need another internal office memo.

From: i-Santander Bank
To: James Veitch

Subject: Internal Office Memo   Date: February 5 10:15 am

Internal Office Memo

Dear Customer,

Sequel to our last correspondence, to complete your application, please kindly fill and return to us the online application form send to you previously.

Please send the account activation deposit fee of 5,200.00 GBP.

We Remain, Mr. Charles Frankfort
(General Director of operations)

From: James Veitch
To: i-Santander Bank

Subject: Re: Internal Office Memo   Date: February 5 3:00 pm

Charles,

How high do the tiers really go? Don't mess with me here. If there's something higher than the **Diamond Reserve Account**, then I want to know about it. Ideally it'd be a **Current Advantage Plus Diamond Reserve**. But I'd settle for a **Current Plus Diamond**. I really think you're restricting yourself with just these four tiers. Is there someone I can speak to about this?

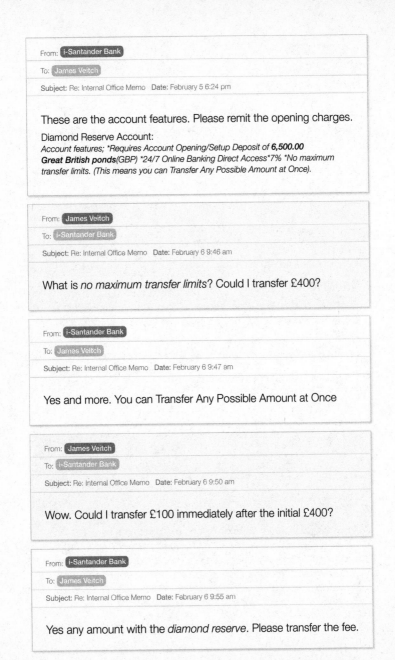

From: **i-Santander Bank**
To: James Veitch
Subject: Re: Internal Office Memo   Date: February 5 6:24 pm

These are the account features. Please remit the opening charges.

Diamond Reserve Account:
*Account features; *Requires Account Opening/Setup Deposit of **6,500.00**
Great British ponds(GBP) *24/7 Online Banking Direct Access*7% *No maximum
transfer limits. (This means you can Transfer Any Possible Amount at Once).*

From: James Veitch
To: i-Santander Bank
Subject: Re: Internal Office Memo   Date: February 6 9:46 am

What is *no maximum transfer limits*? Could I transfer £400?

From: **i-Santander Bank**
To: James Veitch
Subject: Re: Internal Office Memo   Date: February 6 9:47 am

Yes and more. You can Transfer Any Possible Amount at Once

From: James Veitch
To: i-Santander Bank
Subject: Re: Internal Office Memo   Date: February 6 9:50 am

Wow. Could I transfer £100 immediately after the initial £400?

From: **i-Santander Bank**
To: James Veitch
Subject: Re: Internal Office Memo   Date: February 6 9:55 am

Yes any amount with the *diamond reserve*. Please transfer the fee.

From: James Veitch
To: i-Santander Bank

Subject: Re: Internal Office Memo   Date: February 6 10:00 am

Shut up! Let me get this straight. I can transfer any amount?

From: i-Santander Bank
To: James Veitch

Subject: Re: Internal Office Memo   Date: February 6 10:01 am

This is true.

From: James Veitch
To: i-Santander Bank

Subject: Re: Internal Office Memo   Date: February 6 10:01 am

Could I transfer nine and a half pennies?

From: i-Santander Bank
To: James Veitch

Subject: Re: Internal Office Memo   Date: February 6 10:02 am

Yes, is possible with the *diamond reserve account*.

From: James Veitch
To: i-Santander Bank

Subject: Re: Internal Office Memo   Date: February 6 10:04 am

How about 5 million fifty pence pieces? Could I transfer that?

From: i-Santander Bank
To: James Veitch

Subject: Re: Internal Office Memo   Date: February 6 10:05 am

YOU CAN TRANSFER ANY AMOUNT

From: James Veitch
To: i-Santander Bank

Subject: Re: Internal Office Memo   Date: February 6 10:05 am

Ok. And 24/7 online banking. This sounds useful. What is it?

From: i-Santander Bank
To: James Veitch

Subject: Re: Internal Office Memo   Date: February 6 10:06 am

You can access online banking all day and night

From: James Veitch
To: i-Santander Bank

Subject: Re: Internal Office Memo   Date: February 6 10:06 am

All day and all night??

From: i-Santander Bank
To: James Veitch

Subject: Re: Internal Office Memo   Date: February 6 10:06 am

Yes.

From: James Veitch
To: i-Santander Bank

Subject: Re: Internal Office Memo   Date: February 6 10:07 am

I can check my bank account at 3am?

From: i-Santander Bank
To: James Veitch

Subject: Re: Internal Office Memo   Date: February 6 10:07 am

yes.

From: James Veitch
To: i-Santander Bank

Subject: Re: Internal Office Memo   Date: February 6 10:08 am

Impossible! How about at 3:04am almost directly after checking at 3am?

From: i-Santander Bank
To: James Veitch

Subject: Re: Internal Office Memo   Date: February 6 10:08 am

Go away

From: James Veitch
To: i-Santander Bank

Subject: Re: Internal Office Memo   Date: February 6 10:09 am

Sold!

The Meta-Scam

From: Henry McLurkin

To: James Veitch

Subject: COMPENSATION   Date: September 25 3:10 pm

BRITISH HIGH COMMISSION
Henrygote House,
Aguyi Ironsi Street,
Maitama District Lagos, Nigeria.

Dear Scam Victim.

I am Henry McLurkin am a legal practitioner and human rights activist. It was brought to our notice that some people here engage themselves in email scams, hereby extorting money from innocent people online in pretense of Winnings and so on.Your name was among those scammed as listed by the *Nigeria Financial Intelligent Unit*. Your compensation is Three Million United States Dollars. I know this may sound strange and unbelievable to you but it is true.

Subject: Re: COMPENSATION Date: September 25 5:28 pm

Henry, you're 100% right. I was a scam victim. I ended up sending money to people all over the place and nothing ended up coming of it. We never made an investment and, as I predicted, hummus sky-rocketed circa 2011. Question. Is there any way we can hunt down these rascals? I'm willing to travel.

It does sound strange and unbelievable, you're right, but then again, so did Tamagotchis and they were a goer.

From: Henry McLurkin

To: James Veitch

Subject: Re: COMPENSATION Date: September 25 5:55 pm

Dear Scam Victim, Please forward your telephone number, address and other relevant information for comparison with the information we have here to enable us release your fund immediately without delay. Be advised that you should stop further contacts with all the fake lawyers and security companies who in collaboration scammed you.

Henry McLurkin
Legal Practitioner

I'm SO sick of all those fake lawyers, Henry. Telephone: (020) 7774 1000 Address: 16 Ringdonut St., W1 42SFGS

But oh, Henry! First there was my friend Alex and then Godwin and then Mary and Gary and then, well, I can't remember them all but Elena was the latest. Elena was wonderful, Henry; wonderful in a way I can't describe (mostly because we'd never met). But she had that insouciance and selfless disarming charm that we're all after, aren't we Henry?

Anyway, you know they say "'tis better to have loved and lost than never to have loved at all"? Well, whoever said that had clearly not met Elena either. Because it's killing me. I spend whole days in my room listening to 10cc's *I'm Not in Love* and that Feist song *Secret Heart* which is actually better than the original.

I digress. Send me the 3 million. It will be easier to forget her if I have a few houses.

James

I called the number you gave me few minutes ago but the lady on the phone could not understand me.

From: James Veitch
To: Henry McLurkin
Subject: Re: COMPENSATION Date: September 30 6:38 pm

Why could she not understand you? Project!

Sent from my iPhone 4

From: Henry McLurkin
To: James Veitch
Subject: Re: COMPENSATION Date: October 1 6:15 pm

James, I have called you several times and I always get a woman on the phone. What is delaying you? You are required to pay a precessing and documentation fee of $390 through Paypal to Jeremiah Williams.

From: James Veitch
To: Henry McLurkin
Subject: Re: COMPENSATION Date: October 1 6:28 pm

Great. Who's Jeremiah though?

Sent from my iPhone 5

From: Henry McLurkin
To: James Veitch
Subject: Re: COMPENSATION Date: October 3 2:27 pm

That is my name,

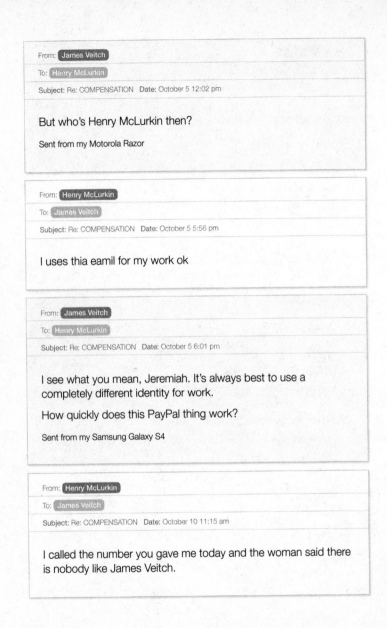

From: James Veitch
To: Henry McLurkin
Subject: Re: COMPENSATION   Date: October 5 12:02 pm

But who's Henry McLurkin then?

Sent from my Motorola Razor

From: Henry McLurkin
To: James Veitch
Subject: Re: COMPENSATION   Date: October 5 5:56 pm

I uses thia eamil for my work ok

From: James Veitch
To: Henry McLurkin
Subject: Re: COMPENSATION   Date: October 5 6:01 pm

I see what you mean, Jeremiah. It's always best to use a completely different identity for work.

How quickly does this PayPal thing work?

Sent from my Samsung Galaxy S4

From: Henry McLurkin
To: James Veitch
Subject: Re: COMPENSATION   Date: October 10 11:15 am

I called the number you gave me today and the woman said there is nobody like James Veitch.

From: James Veitch
To: Henry McLurkin

Subject: Re: COMPENSATION Date: October 10 11:18 am

Are you sure you are phoning the right number?

Sent from my iPhone 14

From: Henry McLurkin
To: James Veitch

Subject: Re: COMPENSATION Date: October 10 11:20 am

She said it was the switchboard of Goldman Sachs bank.

From: James Veitch
To: Henry McLurkin

Subject: Re: COMPENSATION Date: October 10 11:21 am

That's the one!

Sent from my Nokia 5210

From: Henry McLurkin
To: James Veitch

Subject: Re: COMPENSATION Date: October 10 11:34 am

She said she has checked around and there is no such person there.

From: **James Veitch**

To: **Henry McLurkin**

Subject: Re: COMPENSATION   Date: October 10 2:09 pm

How odd because I 100% definitely work there. That's not the sort of thing you make a mistake about. I will have one of my assistants look into this. Are you pronouncing my name right? It's a silent H, T and V.

Sent from my Gameboy Advance

From: **Henry McLurkin**

To: **James Veitch**

Subject: Re: COMPENSATION   Date: October 11 8:06 am

It will interest you to know that nobody is persuading or forcing you to claim your fund.

If you want the fund you must send the documentation fee of $390 through Paypal to Jeremiah Williams.

From: **James Veitch**

To: **Henry McLurkin**

Subject: Re: COMPENSATION   Date: October 11 8:09 am

How quickly does this PayPal thing work?

From: **Henry McLurkin**

To: **James Veitch**

Subject: Re: COMPENSATION   Date: October 11 8:11 am

Is very easy and fast paye online You can log on at www.paypal .com and get your account is very easy to create and safe ok.

From: James Veitch
To: Henry McLurkin
Subject: Re: COMPENSATION   Date: October 11 8:20 am

It just says this when I try to email: "The following address is not valid: 'www.paypal.com'"

From: Henry McLurkin
To: James Veitch
Subject: Re: COMPENSATION   Date: October 11 8:23 am

It is not email address is an website ok. Website is diffrent from email address just register with them ok

---

From: James Veitch
To: Henry McLurkin
Subject: Re: COMPENSATION   Date: October 11 8:26 am

Just so you know, you're blowing my mind right now. It's asking me all sorts of questions like what my mother's maiden name is and I don't know it. Is it ok to call her, do you think?

From: Henry McLurkin
To: James Veitch
Subject: Re: COMPENSATION   Date: October 11 8:30 am

Just put one ok.

Subject: Re: COMPENSATION Date: October 11 8:32 am

But "One" wasn't her maiden name. Or was it? It could have been actually. It would be really weird if you'd just guessed her last name. Have you ever done this sort of thing before? How many fingers am I holding up right now?

From: Henry McLurkin
To: James Veitch

Subject: Re: COMPENSATION Date: October 11 8:41 am

Don't know?

From: James Veitch
To: Henry McLurkin

Subject: Re: COMPENSATION Date: October 11 8:45 am

I wasn't holding any up! I was typing! Which is why you didn't know. You have THE GIFT, Jeremiah. But will you use it for good or ill?

From: James Veitch
To: Henry McLurkin

Subject: Re: COMPENSATION Date: October 11 8:58 am

Have you ever felt like you knew what someone is about to say before they...

From: **Henry McLurkin**

To: **James Veitch**

Subject: Re: COMPENSATION Date: October 11 8:59 am

What

From: **James Veitch**

To: **Henry McLurkin**

Subject: Re: COMPENSATION Date: October 11 9:00 am

Exactly. "Have you ever felt like you knew what someone is about to say before they What."

From: **Henry McLurkin**

To: **James Veitch**

Subject: Re: COMPENSATION Date: October 11 9:13 am

Live me alone go away fuck off man you are just wasting my time

---

From: **James Veitch**

To: **Henry McLurkin**

Subject: Re: COMPENSATION Date: October 11 9:15 am

What? I finally register for PayPal and this is how you treat me?

From: **Henry McLurkin**

To: **James Veitch**

Subject: Re: COMPENSATION Date: October 11 9:17 am

Okay let me have the email use to register wth them?

From: James Veitch
To: Henry McLurkin
Subject: Re: COMPENSATION   Date: October 11 9:21 am

ronaldmcdonald@bingbong.co.uk

From: Henry McLurkin
To: James Veitch
Subject: Re: COMPENSATION   Date: October 11 9:30 am

You are sick

Unattended Item

From: Howard Castallo

To: James Veitch

Subject: YOUR ABANDONED PACKAGE FOR DELIVERY   Date: January 15 10:03 am

Hi, I am Howard Castallo, head of luggage/baggage storage facilities here at the Heathrow International Airport London UK.

I am contacting you regarding an abandoned consignment box in our storage facility. The custom scan report of the box revealed an undisclosed sum of US dollar bill which could be approximately 2-3million dollars.

I have taken it upon myself to contact you personally about this abandoned consignment is because I want us to transact business and share the money 70% for you and 30% for me since the consignment has not yet been returned to the United States.

If you are interested, please reply immediately and observe utmost confidentiality

From: James Veitch

To: Howard Castallo

Subject: Re: YOUR ABANDONED PACKAGE FOR DELIVERY   Date: January 15 10:11 am

You had me at abandoned consignment. What of it?

From: **Howard Castallo**

To: James Veitch

Subject: Re: YOUR ABANDONED PACKAGE FOR DELIVERY   Date: January 15 10:18 am

Dear James Veitch

I,m very happy to read from you. The consignment box was abandoned here by a diplomat who was on transit to your country. Due to lack of proper clearance it is in our storage facility.

I will arrange for the box to be delivered to you or I can bring it myself to ensure a safe delivery. But you have to assure me of my 30% share of the total money in the box.

I wait to hear from you urgently. Regards, Howard Castallo

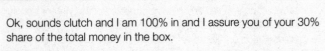

From: **James Veitch**

To: Howard Castallo

Subject: Re: YOUR ABANDONED PACKAGE FOR DELIVERY   Date: January 16 12:21 pm

Ok, sounds clutch and I am 100% in and I assure you of your 30% share of the total money in the box.

What's next? Shall we meet up so I can assure you of your 30% share of the total money in the box in person?

From: **Howard Castallo**

To: James Veitch

Subject: Re: YOUR ABANDONED PACKAGE FOR DELIVERY   Date: January 16 1:00 pm

We will ONLY communicate through email, No meet or telephone conversation to avoid any mistakes.

You must maintain top confidentiality towards this transactions and avoid thirdparty involment to avoid getting me into trrouble of any kind.

From: James Veitch
To: Howard Castallo

Subject: Re: YOUR ABANDONED PACKAGE FOR DELIVERY   Date: January 16 1:30 pm

Understood. We should talk about this though; what's your number?

From: Howard Castallo
To: James Veitch

Subject: Re: YOUR ABANDONED PACKAGE FOR DELIVERY   Date: January 16 1:35 pm

As I said we must communicate ONLY THROUGH EMAIL for security reasons. kindly send me your full detail.

Rest assured that this transaction would be most profitable for both of us.

From: James Veitch
To: Howard Castallo

Subject: Re: YOUR ABANDONED PACKAGE FOR DELIVERY   Date: January 16 2:46 pm

Wonderful. Ok. Sorry about that. Do you have a mobile I can text you on?

Also, sorry for saying "clutch" a few emails ago. I overheard someone say it and it sounded really cool but I'm not sure I can pull it off.

Btw I'm still not 100% clear on what we are doing here. Someone has left this package at the airport and I'm going to leave another one in its place? The ole swaparoo.

No. Read carefully. I will use ur details to prepare way bill and enter it into the delivery manifest and tags thereby presenting you as the beneficiary and receiver of the consignment.

I want you to provide me your full name, phone Number and full address and the nearest airport close to you,

No cell phones or other communication.

Roger that. But Howard, this is gonna blow your mind: the closest airport to me is actually...Heathrow International Airport London UK!!!! The very place where you're head of luggage / baggage storage facilities!

Since you're close I think we should stick with my initial plan.

Rather than changing names on the manifest and whatnot (risky), I suggest I come down there to the luggage/baggage storage facilities and ask to speak to the manager (you). I then check in my consignment box (which happens to look exactly like yours) and then half an hour later I come back and check out the consignment box (less risky). Except instead of giving me my box, you give me the box with the money.

Genius, no?

From: Howard Castallo
To: James Veitch
Subject: Re: YOUR ABANDONED PACKAGE FOR DELIVERY **Date:** January 17 10:11 am

No this will not work.

From: James Veitch
To: Howard Castallo
Subject: Re: YOUR ABANDONED PACKAGE FOR DELIVERY **Date:** January 17 10:56 am

Do you need me to run you through it again? Do you have a fax number I could get you on?

From: Howard Castallo
To: James Veitch
Subject: Re: YOUR ABANDONED PACKAGE FOR DELIVERY **Date:** January 17 10:58 am

I cannot deliver a consignment without securing the delivery clearance under your name, and to enable your details be in the delivery manifest,

---

From: James Veitch
To: Howard Castallo
Subject: Re: YOUR ABANDONED PACKAGE FOR DELIVERY **Date:** January 17 10:58 am

Ok. WhatsApp me to discuss?

From: Howard Castallo

To: James Veitch

Subject: Re: YOUR ABANDONED PACKAGE FOR DELIVERY   Date: January 17 10:59 am

HOW MANY TIMES EMAIL ONLY. NO PHONES. NO FAX. NO
WHATSALP

From: James Veitch

To: Howard Castallo

Subject: Re: YOUR ABANDONED PACKAGE FOR DELIVERY   Date: January 17 11:00 am

Where do you stand on Facebook?

From: Howard Castallo

To: James Veitch

Subject: Re: YOUR ABANDONED PACKAGE FOR DELIVERY   Date: January 17 11:01 am

we are beginning a transaction of millions of dollars and you are
not reading me carefully. now kindly enable me know your true
position and enable me update you on the level of preparation

---

From: Howard Castallo

To: James Veitch

Subject: Re: YOUR ABANDONED PACKAGE FOR DELIVERY   Date: January 18 10:12 am

Dear James i have sent several email to you, but your not
responding to my email. Howard Castallo

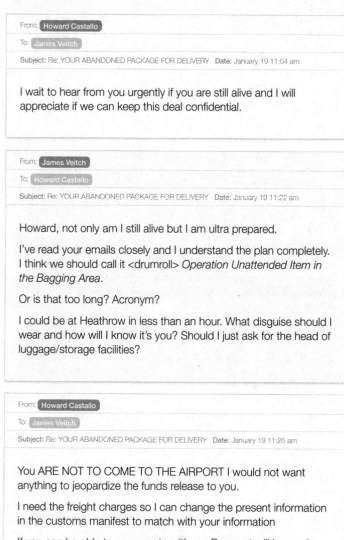

From: Howard Castallo
To: James Veitch
Subject: Re: YOUR ABANDONED PACKAGE FOR DELIVERY Date: January 19 11:04 am

I wait to hear from you urgently if you are still alive and I will appreciate if we can keep this deal confidential.

From: James Veitch
To: Howard Castallo
Subject: Re: YOUR ABANDONED PACKAGE FOR DELIVERY Date: January 19 11:22 am

Howard, not only am I still alive but I am ultra prepared.

I've read your emails closely and I understand the plan completely. I think we should call it <drumroll> *Operation Unattended Item in the Bagging Area*.

Or is that too long? Acronym?

I could be at Heathrow in less than an hour. What disguise should I wear and how will I know it's you? Should I just ask for the head of luggage/storage facilities?

From: Howard Castallo
To: James Veitch
Subject: Re: YOUR ABANDONED PACKAGE FOR DELIVERY Date: January 19 11:25 am

You ARE NOT TO COME TO THE AIRPORT I would not want anything to jeopardize the funds release to you.

I need the freight charges so I can change the present information in the customs manifest to match with your information

If you can be able to co-operate with me Payment will be made under your name to match with the computer printouts.

From: James Veitch
To: Howard Castallo
Subject: Re: YOUR ABANDONED PACKAGE FOR DELIVERY   Date: January 19 11:29 am

Ok. Change the name on the consignment to James Veitch. In fact write "For the attention of James Veitch."

How do I pay these freight charges?

From: Howard Castallo
To: James Veitch
Subject: Re: YOUR ABANDONED PACKAGE FOR DELIVERY   Date: January 19 11:36 am

The actual amount we will spend to get this sorted out is £8,625 Pounds, You wil divide this amount into two and send half through western union money transfer to Netherlands to Peter Kuipers while i start processing the needed documents to effect delivery before 25th of January

Kindly get back to me with further questioning and information.

From: James Veitch
To: Howard Castallo
Subject: Re: YOUR ABANDONED PACKAGE FOR DELIVERY   Date: January 19 11:38 am

Clutch. How do we swap the bags though? Do you have a picture of yours so I can find one that matches? Is it Samsonite? They're quite pricey, so I hope not.

From: Howard Castallo

To: James Veitch

Subject: Re: YOUR ABANDONED PACKAGE FOR DELIVERY **Date:** January 19 11:46 am

There is no swap taking place. If you read my messages you would understand. I am ready to leave this transaction with you if you do not listen. Are you not interested in 2-3million dollars?

When you send the £8,625 Pounds to not jeopardise this business?

From: James Veitch

To: Howard Castallo

Subject: Re: YOUR ABANDONED PACKAGE FOR DELIVERY **Date:** January 19 11:47 am

Ah. Yes. I've read back through the messages and it now makes perfect sense. Sorry to have misunderstood again.

Can I just ask though: you said the bag contained 2–3 million dollars, but can you be more specific? I.e., is it likely to be closer to 3 million or 2 million? I'm concerned a cash injection of 3 million dollars may impact my tax bracket.

From: Howard Castallo

To: James Veitch

Subject: Re: YOUR ABANDONED PACKAGE FOR DELIVERY **Date:** January 19 11:47 am

You must send £8,625 Pounds by Western Union before I can open the box.

From: James Veitch
To: Howard Castallo

Subject: Re: YOUR ABANDONED PACKAGE FOR DELIVERY   Date: January 19 11:48 am

Ok. I'm going to do that tomorrow first thing full stop. Out of interest, what sort of box is it?

From: Howard Castallo
To: James Veitch

Subject: Re: YOUR ABANDONED PACKAGE FOR DELIVERY   Date: January 19 11:49 am

Metal Trunk Box weighing approximately 110kg.

From: James Veitch
To: Howard Castallo

Subject: Re: YOUR ABANDONED PACKAGE FOR DELIVERY   Date: January 20 3:00 pm

Thing is, I don't want to send the money without knowing whether it's 2 million or 3 million.

Perhaps pick it up and shake it around to get a feel for how much is in there.

From: James Veitch
To: Howard Castallo

Subject: Re: YOUR ABANDONED PACKAGE FOR DELIVERY   Date: January 21 8:15 am

Did you shake it?

Subject: Re: YOUR ABANDONED PACKAGE FOR DELIVERY   Date: January 21 10:15 am

Yes. It is closer to three million.

Subject: Re: YOUR ABANDONED PACKAGE FOR DELIVERY   Date: January 21 11:47 am

Awesome.

What does the consignment look like? I'm sort of finding this hard to believe. To be honest, if you could provide a picture it would make it a lot easier.

Western Union tomorrow, 9 am.

Subject: Re: YOUR ABANDONED PACKAGE FOR DELIVERY   Date: January 21 11:55 am

From: James Veitch
To: Howard Castallo
Subject: Re: YOUR ABANDONED PACKAGE FOR DELIVERY   **Date:** January 21 12:07 pm

Seems legit. I can work with that. Give me a few days and I should have something we can use as the dummy for *UIITBA*.

From: Howard Castallo
To: James Veitch
Subject: Re: YOUR ABANDONED PACKAGE FOR DELIVERY   **Date:** January 21 12:08 pm

"UIITBA."

??

From: James Veitch
To: Howard Castallo
Subject: Re: YOUR ABANDONED PACKAGE FOR DELIVERY   **Date:** January 21 12:12 pm

Operation *Unattended Item in the Bagging Area*

If you read my emails closely you would understand.

Working on dummy bag for the swap now. How observant are your staff?

Subject: Re: YOUR ABANDONED PACKAGE FOR DELIVERY   Date: January 21 12:26 pm

You do not need to do anything but pay the expences we are expected to undertake to make this a success

Freight charges according to weight and Destination:
£8,625Pounds Total

It is vital that we are careful right now it may cause me my job,so I need somebody that I can trust for me to be able to review the secret to you.

Subject: Re: YOUR ABANDONED PACKAGE FOR DELIVERY   Date: January 21 12:36 pm

Couldn't agree more. Super careful. The packages must look identical.

We don't want to be into a *Temple of Doom* scenario where we miscalculate the weight of a golden idol. Howard, I'm not saying there'll be arrows, spiders, and boulders (this is Heathrow not Gatwick) but, as you, yourself, say *"we need to avoid getting you into trrouble of any kind."*

I've bought a box for 50p from a thrift store. Looks fairly similar.

Subject: Re: YOUR ABANDONED PACKAGE FOR DELIVERY   Date: January 21 12:37 pm

WE MUST PAY THE FREIGHT CHARGES NOT SWAP BOXES

You do not understand how serious this is.

From: James Veitch
To: Howard Castallo
Subject: Re: YOUR ABANDONED PACKAGE FOR DELIVERY   Date: January 21 12:40 pm

I'm sorry. I do understand. I promise I'm going to go to Western Union tomorrow.

From: Howard Castallo
To: James Veitch
Subject: Re: YOUR ABANDONED PACKAGE FOR DELIVERY   Date: January 21 12:40 pm

Good.

From: Howard Castallo
To: James Veitch
Subject: Re: YOUR ABANDONED PACKAGE FOR DELIVERY   Date: January 22 9:55 am

Am yet to read from u before proceeding

From: James Veitch
To: Howard Castallo

Subject: Re: YOUR ABANDONED PACKAGE FOR DELIVERY   Date: January 22 12:23 pm

Thoughts?

Now, when do we make the exchange? Do you want to call me so we can go over the plan once more?

From: Howard Castallo
To: James Veitch

Subject: Re: YOUR ABANDONED PACKAGE FOR DELIVERY   Date: January 22 12:25 pm

Fuck u

Without Trousers

From: Cpt Scott Bicknall

To: James Veitch

Subject: Good day to you   Date: June 2 12:42 am

I am Capt Scott Bicknall currently serving with the 4th Battalion in United Kingdom.

We have some amount of funds that was cleared in your name. I receive your email and after going through a File. Your File have been approved for payment,

i have been a good British Citizen. I appreciate assisting people and I fight against oppression. Please provide me with a photocopy of your passport.

i decided to render you the best services needed to ensure that your funds get to you easily, Await your swift response-

Your Faithfully,

Capt Scott Bicknall

From: **James Veitch**

To: **Cpt Scott Bicknall**

Subject: Re: Good day to you   Date: June 9 2:22 pm

Captain Bicknall,

A pleasure to make your acquaintance. I am Lieutenant James B. Veitch and I, too, have been a good British Citizen. For the most part. I've had issues with my TV license but, in my defense, the rules are super hard to understand. I'm also no stranger to fighting oppression, so there's that too.

Why do you need my passport? I'm a bit reticent to hand that over. Last time I gave my passport out was to a Crimean chap who ended up claiming all the points on my nectar card.

From: **Cpt Scott Bicknall**

To: **James Veitch**

Subject: Re: Good day to you   Date: June 10 2:48 pm

Dear Lieutenant Veitch,

We need to get you am account to you can transfer to your local bank. we need your details please

thanks

Capt Scott Bicknall

From: **James Veitch**

To: **Cpt Scott Bicknall**

Subject: Re: Good day to you   Date: June 10 8:42 pm

Captain Scott,

Which details do you need exactly, and how hard must we fight oppression? Can you tell me about how you've been fighting oppression, and how hard you fought?

To: James Veitch

Subject: Re: Good day to you Date: June 11 3:08 pm

We must fight oppression very hard.

You need to send me your Names: Address: Sex: Age, Country, Mobile number and a passport copy to enable me proceed with the confirmation of your funds release.

From: James Veitch

To: Cpt Scott Bicknall

Subject: Re: Good day to you Date: June 11 3:16 pm

Cap,

I'll send the details over at oh eight hundred hours (before breakfast) tomorrow.

On a personal note; I must thank you for getting in touch. I've missed the military and long believed my court-martial and dishonorable discharge was a travesty of justice.

Now, tell me all about this money. And this oppression. I'm glad to hear we're on the same team.

I've given you all my details. What's holding this whole shebang up?

From: Cpt Scott Bicknall

To: James Veitch

Subject: Re: Good day to you Date: June 11 3:27 pm

We are together. We are military men fighting oppression. It is what you and I both stand for. Please follow this link and put in your bank details and password for the release of your funds

http://   .com

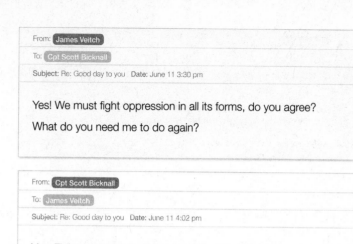

From: James Veitch
To: Cpt Scott Bicknall
Subject: Re: Good day to you   **Date:** June 11 3:30 pm

Yes! We must fight oppression in all its forms, do you agree?

What do you need me to do again?

From: Cpt Scott Bicknall
To: James Veitch
Subject: Re: Good day to you   **Date:** June 11 4:02 pm

Yes. Fight opression in all the forms it comes by.

Click on the link put in all the details it asks for including your bankusername and password to verify with your bank that you have the money we are sending.

From: James Veitch
To: Cpt Scott Bicknall
Subject: Re: Good day to you   **Date:** June 11 4:06 pm

On the site now. It's asking for my bank, username, email address, password, and security key.

Captain, I ask you, can a man who obeys all orders truly be said to be a man?

From: Cpt Scott Bicknall
To: James Veitch
Subject: Re: Good day to you   **Date:** June 11 4:09 pm

No he is not a man.

Yes please, and full in your details too thanks so much

From: Cpt Scott Bicknall

To: James Veitch

Subject: Re: Good day to you   Date: June 11 4:17 pm

Not fair.

Just put your email and password and bank details. thank so much

From: James Veitch

To: Cpt Scott Bicknall

Subject: Re: Good day to you   Date: June 11 4:19 pm

Why is it that when a soldier marches for his country it is heroic, yet when he does so without trousers it is "wholly inappropriate" for the Diamond Jubilee?

Ok. My email is james@   .com, right?

From: Cpt Scott Bicknall

To: James Veitch

Subject: Re: Good day to you   Date: June 11 4:48 pm

what about your password. please add your password and a other information.

Yes. I'm doing that.

Do you agree I should be allowed to not wear trousers? Captain?

I do not know. Yes no trousers.

Captain Bicknall. Brother. As I fill in these personal and highly confidential bank details on an unencrypted site I do not recognize, I ask you to make me a promise, nay, a pledge...

Captain. If push came to shove, would you stand with me, trouser-less, shoulder to shoulder, thigh to thigh, legs quivering in the wind as rosy fingered dawn broke over Buckingham Palace? Would you?

Please you funds is ready now. when you are ready for it just put your email other details to release it

From: James Veitch
To: Cpt Scott Bicknall

Subject: Re: Good day to you   Date: June 12 1:00 pm

Would you, Captain? Would you do that for me?

From: Cpt Scott Bicknall
To: James Veitch

Subject: Re: Good day to you   Date: June 12 1:00 pm

Yes

From: James Veitch
To: Cpt Scott Bicknall

Subject: Re: Good day to you   Date: June 12 1:16 pm

Good.

Now. Any idea what my password could be?

What's yours? Perhaps I have the same one.

From: Cpt Scott Bicknall
To: James Veitch

Subject: Re: Good day to you   Date: June 12 1:16 pm

You think this is a funny game?

From: James Veitch
To: Cpt Scott Bicknall

Subject: Re: Good day to you   Date: June 12 1:17 pm

Ummmm yes :)

Dora

Subject: Honest and sincere **Date:** February 19 12:15 pm

Dear Friend

I got your contact from a South African NGO health officer Miss Dora Myunga in Accra Ghana. She described you as an honest and kind person. This motivated me to send you this mail.

I was asoldier but unfortunately I am wanted by the new leader of my country.

I need a foreign assistance to move Carats of

polished Diamond.

I will give you 40% of the total Money and Diamond. I am not a greedy

person and want you to be honest and sincere in this transaction.

To confirm you are interested to execute this transaction, I need the following:

Nationality...
Fax/Phone Number...
Your Date of Birth..
Marital Status...
Place of Birth..

but because of my involvement in the war. The leader of my country

dose not has knowledge of this money and diamond. Please keep this information secret.

Thank you.

Regards,
Lt. Kamanda Koroma

From: James Veitch
To: Kamanda Koroma
Subject: Re: Honest and sincere   Date: February 19 12:21 pm

Dear Lieutenant Kamanda,

I was very surprised to get this email. I don't recall Miss Dora Myunga; how did she say we met?

Yours,
Dr. James Veitch MD

From: Kamanda Koroma
To: James Veitch
Subject: Re: Honest and sincere   Date: February 19 12:50 pm

Dear Dr Veitch,

Thank you for candid effort to respond to my mail, well I did not ask Miss Dora how you people met, but she said that it's been a long time it happened.

But the most important for me is that I can trust you to work with you, as you know that the only thing I really needed is a trustworthy person.

Do try and communicate me your full details, so that we shall quickly proceed.

Regards,
Lt Kamanda.

From: James Veitch

To: Kamanda Koroma

Subject: Re: Honest and sincere   Date: February 20 8:06 am

Dear Lt. Kamanda,

I have just received your email. Was Dora a small woman? I think I remember her.

Yes, you can trust me. Here are my details.

Nationality: British
Fax/Phone Number: 0207 774 1000
Your Date of Birth: 1/04/1907
Marital Status: Single
Place of Birth: Hampstead Heath

Yours, Dr. James Veitch

From: Kamanda Koroma

To: James Veitch

Subject: Re: Honest and sincere   Date: February 20 11:00 am

Dear Dr. James,

Thanks a lot for your mail, yes miss Dora is somewhat small in stature.

She gave me an assurance that you are an honest man, and I am so much happy about that.

You will contact the security Company HillSide Safe Keeping Company in Ghana and introduce yourself as my foreign partner as soon as possible. Tell the Company that you want them to deliver the consignment to you.

Regards,
Lt Kamanda.

From: James Veitch

To: Kamanda Koroma

Subject: Re: Honest and sincere   Date: February 20 11:30 am

I'll contact HillSide Safe Keeping Company in Ghana first thing tomorrow morning. But Kamanda—may I call you that?—I'm concerned we are not talking about the same Dora at all and I would hate to find out this was all some misunderstanding. How small are we talking? The Dora I knew was very small indeed. She was roughly the height of a Shetland pony. Can you confirm?

I'm cc-ing the consultancy firm in on this. Can you confirm what investment I will be receiving?

Happy doing business with you.

From: Kamanda Koroma

To: James Veitch

Subject: Re: Honest and sincere   Date: February 21 11:44 am

Dear James,

Thanks a lot for your mail, actually I cannot be able to get the full picture of how small Miss Dora is in my memory right at this moment. But all I could remember is that she's not all that a big stature person

But does not really matter to me at all, what matters to me is that I could remember vividly that she told me that you are very very honest person.

It's been a very long time we met, but her good advice is still ringing bell in my heart and in my head. Which is the reason while I am so comfortable in working with you.

I tried to call you yesterday with the phone number you gave me, but a lady picked up the phone and told me that it was a wrong number. I will be waiting to hear from you sooner.

Regards,
Lt Kamanda.

Kamanda,

How odd. That's definitely my number.

Meanwhile, I've been asked for a "certificate" for the consignment. Can you provide one for me? I'm also not exactly sure what the consignment is.

I'm so sorry to do this again, but it's vital we make sure we are talking about the same Dora. I want to make 100% certain I am your man.

To be brutally honest, I think I may have somewhat exaggerated her size. She is considerably smaller. I knew her when I was younger and, obviously, when you're small, everything looks bigger. Objectively, I can't see her being much larger than Paddington Bear. Can you confirm?

As long as this is how you remember her, I'm happy to go ahead with the transaction. Long shot, but do you accept Western Union?

Yours,
James

Dear Dr. James,

I called the telephone you gave me again and a lady picked it and said that she did not know anybody with the name Veitch.

I was a bit confused and somewhat worried, could you please give me your direct phone numbers?

We are in for a very serious business, this is not a child's play kind of thing.

Regards,
Lt Kamanda.

From: James Veitch

To: Kamanda Koroma

Subject: Re: Honest and sincere **Date:** February 24 4:22 pm

Lt,

I apologize; you may have got through to the Goldman Sachs switchboard. They know me as Jimmy V at the bank, which is probably why the switchboard didn't know I was there.

Can you give me the certificate that I need? Otherwise I cannot proceed with this business. I haven't heard from you in days and this is making me very concerned.

From: Kamanda Koroma

To: James Veitch

Subject: Re: Honest and sincere **Date:** February 25 12:00 pm

Dear Dr, James,

Thanks for your concern. I called the phone numbers you gave me, and the lady that picked up the phone told me that it's Bank phone and that she did not know you.

I need to talk with you before we can proceed. We are in here for a very very serious business.

Regards,
Lt Kamanda.

From: James Veitch

To: Kamanda Koroma

Subject: Re: Honest and sincere **Date:** February 25 12:30 pm

Kamanda,

I trust you implicitly, but the bank is getting well lairy about this certificate.

Can you please send to me immediately?

Yours, JV MD.

To: James Veitch

Subject: Re: Honest and sincere   Date: February 25 2:20 pm

Dear Dr, James,

When will you be answering phonecalls I have been making or call me on the number I have given you.

Regards,
Lt Kamanda.

From: James Veitch

To: Kamanda Koroma

Subject: Re: Honest and sincere   Date: February 26 10:10 am

Apologies. I have been exceptionally busy seeing patients.

Honestly, I can't get the certificate from you and the other guy is being difficult. I don't know what the consignment is. I'm beginning to think this might be one of those scams you hear so much about.

Dr. J

From: Kamanda Koroma

To: James Veitch

Subject: Re: Honest and sincere   Date: February 26 1:30 pm

Dr James,

I am not sure you are real at all, you gave me phone numbers of a Bank which I called and they say that you are not real, that they don't know you, they even advised me to be very careful about you.

Now you suddenly turn to be a medical doctor seeing patients. And you can't call me?

WHO ARE YOU??????????????? I am an Army Intelligent.

From: James Veitch
To: Kamanda Koroma
Subject: Re: Honest and sincere   Date: February 26 7:55 pm

Dear Kamanda,

There was never a shred of doubt in my mind that I was dealing with an intelligent.

To answer your questions, I see patients during the mornings and hold an advisory position at Goldman Sachs in the afternoons.

How can I prove to you that I am real?

How can you prove that you are real?

In truth, how can any of us prove that we are real?

I also golf professionally.

From: Kamanda Koroma
To: James Veitch
Subject: Re: Honest and sincere   Date: February 28 11:59 am

Dr James.

Hope all is well with you in that part of the world? haven't really heard from you so lately. Please do try and write me my friend. I will await your mail.

Regards,

Lt Kamanda.

From: **James Veitch**

To: **Kamanda Koroma**

Subject: Re: Honest and sincere   Date: February 29 11:28 am

Kamanda,

All is going well here, thank you. I would like a picture of the consignment, please. What does it consist of? What do you need from me to complete this transaction?

From: **Kamanda Koroma**

To: **James Veitch**

Subject: Re: Honest and sincere   Date: February 29 11:32 am

Dr. James,

I will ask the Security Company to take the photo of the consignment and send to me, so that i will forward it to you by mail.

While you and I will use it for investment in Europe. Do send me any of your Valid ID by e-mail attachment. I will await your reply soon.

Regards,
Lt Kamanda.

From: James Veitch
To: Kamanda Koroma

Subject: Re: Honest and sincere   Date: February 29 11:38 am

Kamanda,

I will have my secretary scan my passport and driver's license for me.

In the meantime, please find attached my Blockbuster video membership card.

From: Kamanda Koroma
To: James Veitch

Subject: Re: Honest and sincere   Date: February 29 12:26 pm

Dr. James,

Do try and send me your passport or your driver license. We need to pay off the demur rages before I can have access to the box.

I have forwarded the certificate of deposit to the safekeeping Company, so you have to contact them now and ask them to make delivery to you.

Regards,
Lt Kamanda.

Subject: Re: Honest and sincere   Date: February 29 12:40 pm

Kamanda,

Superb. This is GREAT news. I'll contact the safekeeping company now and get them to send me the bling.

Look, Kamanda, can you take care of the fees and I'll pay you back as soon as I've received the gems?

Subject: Re: Honest and sincere   Date: February 29 12:44 pm

Dr. James,

I did not have any money with me here, which was the reason while I contacted you to assist me make the clearance of the consignment.

Please do try and assist me make the clearance of the consignment. The safekeeping Company called me yesterday and said that you are asking them to open the box before you can be able to proceed. If the safekeeping finds out that the contents of the box is money and diamonds they will confiscate it, because it was deposited as family valuables not as money.

Regards,
Lt Kamanda.

Subject: Re: Honest and sincere   Date: February 29 1:04 pm

Lt Kamanda,

That's fine. How much do you need?

From: Kamanda Koroma
To: James Veitch
Subject: Re: Honest and sincere   Date: February 29 1:14 pm

Dr, James,

Thank you for your mail. I just called the safekeeping Security Company Director now and he told me that he has already told you the amount needed to be paid to them to enable them process the needful documents to be able to deliver the box to your address.

Please Dr. do try and assist me. I really wanted to be out of this place, i am suffering so much here. Please help me.

Regards,
Lt Kamanda.

From: James Veitch
To: Kamanda Koroma
Subject: Re: Honest and sincere   Date: February 29 4:00 pm

Of course. I'm excited to get the consignment. I'm going to pay the money in the next few hours. There's a Western Union really close by.

From: James Veitch
To: Kamanda Koroma
Subject: Re: Honest and sincere   Date: March 3 10:30 am

Kamanda, I tried to send it today, but they said I need some sort of number from you. Or a password or something. Can you help?

From: James Veitch
To: Kamanda Koroma

Subject: Re: Honest and sincere   Date: March 3 5:05 pm

Kamanda,

When can I expect to receive the shipment?

Do you need anything else from me?

I am anxious to get this resolved today as I am going on holiday tomorrow.

From: Kamanda Koroma
To: James Veitch

Subject: Re: Honest and sincere   Date: March 4 11:48 am

Okay give them this as the password. You are Ewu, or ogologo amu. please do that as soon as possible, the company is waiting.

Regards,
Lt Kamanda.

From: James Veitch
To: Kamanda Koroma

Subject: Re: Honest and sincere   Date: March 4 12:38 pm

Will do this tomorrow. What does "ogologo" mean?

From: Kamanda Koroma
To: James Veitch

Subject: Re: Honest and sincere   Date: March 4 12:39 pm

Ogologo means a fine thing. Pls do.

Dr. James, what happen I did not hear from you again, what happened? all hope is well with you.

Thank you for your kind words, Lieutenant. Hearing from you again is an "ogologo"!

When can I expect to receive the shipment?

As I have said you must send the money before I can access the box.

Ah, yes. I completely forgot. I'll do that momentarily.

From: **Kamanda Koroma**

To: **James Veitch**

Subject: Re: Honest and sincere   Date: March 6 10:35 am

Have you sent money?

From: **James Veitch**

To: **Kamanda Koroma**

Subject: Re: Honest and sincere   Date: March 6 2:30 pm

I was about to, Kamanda; I was literally in the queue at Western Union, about to send some cash your way when I realized I'm still not sure that we are talking about the same Dora. The one I knew was quite literally the size of a postage stamp. Can you confirm this?

Coda

From: James Veitch

To: Solomon Oddonkoh

Subject: (no subject) **Date:** January 30 5:44 pm

Solomon, I expect you've sussed out that I've known from the start that you're a scammer. And you know that I know that you know. So I was wondering whether you'd be willing to do an interview with me about what it's like to be a scammer?

From: Solomon Oddonkoh

To: James Veitch

Subject: Re: (no subject) **Date:** January 30 10:13 pm

i cannot believe i have been wasting my precious airtime with a mad man like you. What a waste is this?

You are a total disgrace to manhood.

Go fuck yourself..

fuck you asshole.

Acknowledgments

For Ma, Alan & Hannah

I'm grateful to a ton of people who've made this happen. So, thanks (in the order people come to mind—make of that what you will) to David Pogue for finding it funny enough for the *New York Times*, Charley Elliott and Max Shapira for the title, the French House, ramen and friendship, Gemma Corby because I miss her, Rebecca Soboti for a face and a fly, Fran Bushe for writing on a banana, Annabelle Berizzi, Claudia Laing, Lucia Brizzi and Lynsey-Anne Moffat for boundless enthusiasm, Tom Lamont for believing in it and me, Harry Hill for his generosity, Ed Griffiths and Lucinda Nicholson for being amazing, Joel Parsons for being insanely great, Robert Forknall for being marooned and Hannah Boyde for letting me know. Alex Kern, of course, whose hacked email account inadvertently began everything. Thanks to Matthew Harvey for being an exceptional agent, Winnie Mandela for stirring it up, Carla & Sophia Oddy for their art, my father for his support, Adam Barnard for suggesting I go to print and whomever mans the switchboard at Goldman Sachs for enduring God knows what. Thanks to RHM for beginning with the eyes. Big, massive thanks are due to Céline Hughes, Matilda Forbes Watson, Mollie Weisenfeld, Sarah Falter, Michael Barrs, Monica Oluwek, Fred Francis, Vicky O'Connell, LeAnn Falciani, Sabrina Taitz and the rest of the brilliant team at Hachette Books. Thank you to CB for having made my heart beat a little faster and to Jim Nolan for being the kindest person I know. And thank you, Solomon. Corresponding with you was a treat.

About the Author

Comedian and writer **James Veitch** is renowned for his unashamedly nerdy and hilarious stand-up material. A former Apple Store Genius, Veitch's comedy is high-tech: picking apart, parodying (and pranking) the fast-advancing and perplexing technology we live with. His live shows have explored technology, retro-gaming and finding love through troubleshooting theory.

James has sold out shows throughout the world as well as given three TED Talks—one of which is the most-viewed video on their YouTube channel. He currently holds the third most popular talk of all time on TED.com. He has written and performed two viral hit seasons of his show *Scamalot* with Mashable, made two appearances on TBS's *Conan* and also supported Conan O'Brien on his national tour in 2018. James made his first appearance on *The Tonight Show with Jimmy Fallon* in March 2019 and hosted the BAFTA Britannia Awards in October 2019. He recently filmed his first stand-up special at the Avalon Theater in Los Angeles, produced by Conan O'Brien and Conaco, which will air on HBO Max in 2020.